*Poverty in pre-Famine Westmeath*

# Maynooth Studies in Local History

SERIES EDITOR Michael Potterton

You are reading one of the six volumes in the Maynooth Studies in Local History (MSLH) series for 2023. A benefit of being the editor of this series is the early opportunity to read a very wide variety of bite-sized histories covering events and activities from the magnificent to the outrageous in every nook and cranny of this remarkable island. This year's offerings take us from Bronze Age burials in west Kerry to a three-year dairy war in 1930s east Donegal, via an entrepreneur extraordinaire from late Georgian Cork, a revelatory survey of dire poverty in pre-Famine Westmeath, a century of exclusive terrace-life in colourful Tralee and the complex social networks of a family of Francophile Catholic landed gentry from Kildare. Together, these six studies take us on an astonishing journey on which we encounter smugglers, umbrella makers, lifelike automata, difficult marriage- and education choices, resolute defiance, agrarian violence, rapidly changing religious and political landscapes and a petition to have a region transferred from one nation to another.

These half-a-dozen volumes show how the 'local' focus of a *local history* can range from an individual person (Marsden Haddock) to a family (the Mansfields), a street (Day Place), a village (Portmagee), a county (Donegal and Westmeath) and beyond. The six authors have taken their stories from relative obscurity to centre stage. Denis Casey now joins Terence Dooley as one of only two people to have published three volumes in this series (though they are set to be joined by a third in 2024!).

This year in the Department of History at Maynooth University we are celebrating seventy years of excellence in teaching, research and publication (1953–2023) and we are especially delighted to be relaunching our enormously successful MA in Local History. Theses from this programme have traditionally provided the backbone of the MSLH series and we look forward to another rich crop in the years to come.

Whether you ask Alexa, ChatGPT or Raymond Gillespie, there is no doubting that Local History is valuable and significant. AI has evolved considerably since I grew up on a dairy farm in south Co. Meath and it is sure to play an increasing role in the research, writing and dissemination of local history. As with so many new technologies, of course, the greatest challenge is perhaps going to be maximizing the potential of Artificial Intelligence without compromising the integrity of the results.

*Maynooth Studies in Local History: Number 161*

# Poverty in pre-Famine Westmeath: the findings of the Poor Commission of 1833

Seán Byrne

FOUR COURTS PRESS

Set in 11.5pt on 13.5pt Bembo by
Carrigboy Typesetting Services for
FOUR COURTS PRESS LTD
7 Malpas Street, Dublin 8, Ireland
www.fourcourtspress.ie
*and in North America for*
FOUR COURTS PRESS
c/o IPG, 814 N Franklin Street, Chicago, IL 60610

ISBN 978-1-80151-094-3

Printed in Ireland
by SprintPrint, Dublin

# Contents

# Acknowledgments

I wish to acknowledge the encouragement and advice of Michael Potterton, series editor of Maynooth Studies in Local History, Colm Lennon, Professor Emeritus of History, Maynooth University, historian Ciarán McCabe and my wife Maedhbh McNamara.

# Introduction

As Timothy O'Neill argues, the scale of the Great Famine of 1846 has tended to overshadow the extreme poverty in Ireland in the period 1815–45.[1] There had been several lesser famines during that period and industrial employment declined sharply. At least two million people lived in dire poverty and thousands died in the frequently occurring epidemics of diseases, particularly typhus. While economic conditions deteriorated between 1815 and 1845, population increased rapidly. A system of land tenure that encouraged subdivision of farms, the collapse of the linen and woollen industries after the Act of Union, which instituted free trade between Ireland and England, and the failure to develop other manufacturing industries were major factors contributing to impoverishment in Ireland. Visitors to Ireland in the 1820s and 1830s were shocked by the level of destitution they encountered. Wriothesley Noel, an English Evangelical Protestant clergyman, toured the Irish midlands in 1836 and commented that 'No class on earth is to be more pitied, except it be the North American Indians'.[2] Gustave de Beaumont, a French magistrate and prison reformer, visited Ireland in 1837 and wrote

> I have seen the Indian in his forests, and the Negro in his chains, and thought, as I contemplated their pitiable condition, that I saw the very extreme of human wretchedness; but I did not then know the condition of unfortunate Ireland … In all countries, more or less, paupers may be discovered; but an entire nation of paupers is what was never seen until it was shown in Ireland.[3]

From the 1820s onwards, in the wake of famines and epidemics and an increase in agrarian violence, Ireland's poverty became a major issue in the British parliament and, with the election of more MPs sympathetic to the Irish poor after Catholic Emancipation in 1829, pressure mounted on the British government to address Irish poverty. In 1833 the government established a Royal Commission for inquiring into the condition of the poorer classes. The commission conducted a comprehensive investigation into poverty in Ireland, including holding public hearings in seventeen counties, in which a parish in each barony of those counties was chosen for inquiry. A full account of those public sessions was included in appendices to the reports of the commission and provides an extraordinarily detailed account of life in 1830s Ireland.

This book uses the findings of the Poor Inquiry for Co. Westmeath, and other contemporary sources, to give an account of economic and social conditions in the county in the decade before the Famine.

# 1. Underdevelopment and poverty in Ireland, 1800–36

*The commission of enquiry into the poorer classes in Ireland*, which reported in 1836 and 1837,[1] was established because of the UK government's concern at the alarming extent of extreme poverty in Ireland and the rapid increase in the numbers living in such poverty. Official statistics and accounts by visitors to Ireland in the period 1815 to 1833 paint a picture of destitution among a large part of the population. The population of Ireland quadrupled between 1740 and 1845. The increase was most rapid between 1750 and 1815 and while the growth-rate declined a little after 1815, it remained high compared to other European countries. The census of 1821 recorded a population of 6.8 million while the 1831 census recorded 7.8 million. These figures suggest that the population increased by 1 million or 14.2 per cent in the decade 1831–41. The 1841 census recorded a population of 8.1 million. Joseph Lee argues that the censuses of 1821 and 1831 underestimated the population which he puts at 7.9 million in 1831.[2] Lee's figures give a more credible estimate of the increase in population between 1821 and 1831 of 0.7 million or 10 per cent. This increase was among the highest in Europe for the period and the greatest increase was recorded among landless labourers.

The period 1780 to 1820 saw a rapid increase in Irish agricultural output mainly of wheat, barley and oats due to the adoption of crop rotation, the seed drill and the horse hoe.[3] Despite some mechanization of agriculture during this period, the increased output of crops required an increased agricultural labour force. In Britain, this labour force largely consisted of labourers paid a money wage by landlords and large tenant farmers, while in Ireland the system of cottier labourer developed because of the structure of land ownership. Landlords leased their land to sub-landlords or middlemen who in turn leased it in ever smaller units to small farmers. At the bottom of this pyramid were landless labourers who leased very small plots of land under a year-to-year system known as 'conacre'. James Ebenezer Bicheno, who would become a member of the Poor Commission, understood the conditions of the Irish poor, having toured Ireland in 1829. In a minority report to the commission's third report, Bicheno wrote:

> The most prevalent meaning of a cottier is that of a labourer holding a cabin, either with or without land, as it may happen (but commonly from a quarter to three acres are attached) from a farmer or other occupier for whom he is bound to work, either constantly at a fixed price (usually a very low one), or whenever called upon, or so many days of the week in certain busy seasons, according to the custom of the neighbourhood, the convenience of the landlord or other local or personal circumstances.[4]

Having discharged his labour obligation to his farmer landlord, the labourer could devote the rest of his time to cultivating his own crop, usually potatoes, though occasionally oats or flax, or by working for his farmer landlord or other employer for a money wage. The labourer sold most of the crop to pay the rent and hoped that it might realize a profit, on which he and his family could survive. As the number of labourers rose, and competition for land increased, the rent paid by the labourer to the tenant farmer was often a multiple per acre of what the farmer paid to the landlord. The evidence suggests that labourers employed directly by landlords on land they farmed themselves were better paid and better housed than the cottier-labourers and renters of conacre.[5]

As the number of agricultural labourers grew more rapidly than demand for their labour in the early nineteenth century, ever greater numbers, unable to find work from farmers for which their nominal wage would pay their rent, were driven into the precarious conacre system. Those labourers rented a piece of manured land and grew potatoes or oats on it in the hope that they would be able to sell the crop for a price that would pay the rent and have a little over on which to live. The increase in the numbers of the poorest was made possible by the potato.[6] Potatoes are a high-yielding crop and the only single cheap food that can provide most of the essential nutrients. Supplemented with buttermilk, potatoes provided an almost adequate diet. Enough potatoes to feed a family of six people could be grown on an acre of land. Smallholders divided their land among their children and colonized wasteland that in turn was subdivided. A high-yielding if unpalatable potato variety called the 'lumper' could be grown on marginal land where no other crop would thrive. Potatoes were also fed to pigs, hens, horses and cows and were the lynchpin of the whole tillage system, without which the large-scale production of corn would not have been possible. By the 1830s, at least half a million labourers were struggling to survive on 13 per cent of the agricultural land and, by the standard of the rest of the UK, they were destitute, being often on the brink of starvation for at least part of the period from May to October when the previous year's potatoes had been consumed and before the new crop could be harvested.

The ease with which the cottier-labourer could create a livelihood led to early marriage and large families among this class, in contrast to the farmers who were required to provide a dowry for a daughter, leading to later and fewer marriages and smaller families among farmers. The proportion of labourers to farmers rose rapidly to the point where labourers' wages were driven to subsistence level.

The problems of Irish agriculture were compounded by the fact that Irish landlords were more improvident, evicted more often and took less interest in their land than their English counterparts.[7] Absentee Irish landlords who spent most of their time in England tried to maintain lifestyles like their English peers on lower incomes, which meant they saved little and frequently contracted large debts to fund house-building, winning elections, lawsuits and gambling and hunting. As Joel Mokyr argues, 'Irish landlords were alienated from their tenants, from the land and from agriculture in all its technical and economic aspects'.[8] One quarter of landlords were absentees and one tenth of all estates and a quarter of the estates of absentees were encumbered by debt. Between £2 and £3 million in rents to absentee landlords was leaving Ireland annually by the 1840s.[9]

Irish agriculture prospered during the Napoleonic wars from 1802 to 1815, which increased demand for Irish-produced food, leading to increased prosperity for farmers and labourers. The end of the wars in 1815 led to a sharp fall in demand for Irish-produced food and a fall in prices. An economic depression in Britain in 1819 led to a crisis in Ireland in 1820. Partial failures of the potato crop in 1817 and 1822 led to famine conditions in parts of the country. The crop failure was compounded by low commodity prices due to the ending of wartime demand and bank failures. Another severe depression occurred in 1825–6, which largely affected the textile industry, particularly wool manufacture. The depression in Ireland reflected a severe downturn in the British economy, the worst since 1800. The Irish woollen and cotton industries were also severely affected by cheap imports from the UK. Hundreds of thousands of workers who earned part or all of their incomes from spinning and weaving in their own homes were made redundant. The expansion of the linen industry in the north partly compensated for the loss of jobs in the woollen and cotton industries. In the rest of the country, while the production of woollen fabric recovered somewhat, the redundant cotton workers added to the swelling numbers living in poverty.

The abolition of the Irish parliament by the Act of Union of 1800 removed the possibility of Ireland imposing tariffs on textiles imported from England to protect the Irish textile industry. While some historians saw the Act of Union as a major cause of Ireland's failure to develop industry, Cormac Ó Gráda argues that the decline of Irish industry was caused by rapid industrialization in the UK and that free trade only accelerated a trend that was inevitable.[10]

The growth of population, particularly among landless labourers and the holders of very small farms, and the decline of domestic textile production led to Ireland in the 1830s being more rural and agricultural than it had been in 1800. In contrast to Britain, where in the period 1800 to 1830 the urban population increased sharply as the industrial revolution proceeded, in Ireland few towns other than Dublin and Belfast expanded, and many stagnated.

The *Report of the commission of enquiry into the poorer classes* (1836) noted that there were more agricultural labourers in Ireland than in England and that there were double the number relative to the cultivable land, and four times the number relative to agricultural output.[11] The average agricultural wage in Ireland was 2s. to 2s. 6d. per week, while in Britain it was 8s. to 10s. The commission estimated that there were 585,000 people out of work and 'in distress' for up to thirty weeks. When the dependants of these workers were included, 2.9 million people experienced want for at least three months of the year.

The relentless growth of population and the lack of urban employment due to the failure to industrialize led to a high level of emigration. Between 1815 and 1845, Irish emigrants constituted one tenth of all the people who had gone to the US from Europe from the time of Columbus.[12] One and a half million people left between 1815 and 1845, which represented half of the natural increase in population in that period. Some of this emigration was subsidised by landlords alarmed by the increase in population and subsequent poverty on their estates. Emigration constituted a drain of enterprise as the more enterprising were more likely to emigrate.[13]

Visitors to Ireland in the early years of the nineteenth century were shocked by the poverty of Irish rural labourers, many of whom were barefoot, dressed in rags and living in mud-walled huts. In 1841, 40 per cent of houses were one-roomed cabins. The Irish labourers were able to survive in their mud-walled cabins in winter because they had an abundant supply of cheap fuel in turf. Ó Gráda argues that potatoes and turf were, in a sense, substitutes for better housing and clothing.[14]

The French writer Gustave de Beaumont, who accompanied Alexis de Tocqueville on his tour of England and Ireland in the 1830s, described conditions in the country in his book, *Ireland: social, political and religious* (1839).[15] He commented that 'in every nation there are poor people, more or less numerous, but an entire nation of paupers is something never witnessed before'.[16] Henry Inglis, who visited Ireland in the 1830s, was a travel writer and social commentator who had published accounts of his travels in several other European countries. In 1836 Inglis published *A journey throughout Ireland during the spring, summer and autumn of 1834*. He visited most of the counties in Ireland and provides a great deal of information on economic and social conditions in the places he visited. He found conditions in Ireland worse than in any other country he had visited.[17]

Commenting on the conditions of labourers, he described finding 'a filthy hovel filled with squalid and ragged children, greedily scrambling for a dry potato' and meeting 'women who are begging a few potatoes from the farmers, and if I return with them, I find they are carrying the potatoes home to an infirm mother or father; or husband out of work, or famishing children'.

Inglis compared the houses of the labourers with those of their contemporaries he had seen in Spain. In Callan, Co. Kilkenny, Inglis saw people 'crawling out of their hovels not one shade better than I have seen in the sierras of Granada where the people live in holes excavated in the bank. Their cabins were mere holes with nothing in them except a little straw and one or two broken stools'.[18] Inglis found the people of Callan 'either in a state of actual starvation or barely keeping body and soul together'.[19]

Though Inglis did not visit Westmeath, he visited the neighbouring county of Longford where economic conditions would have been similar. He was taken aback by the state of agriculture in Longford, where he found 'a lamentable want of good husbandry. Nowhere is visible any of the neatness and care which are indicative of industrious habit'.[20] Inglis noted that in Longford wages were 8*d.* per day in summer and 6*d.* in winter and was not surprised to find that labourers did not work very hard. He wondered 'how would an English labourer work if a scanty meal of dry potatoes were substituted for bacon and beer'.[21] Inglis observed that there were few grocery shops in rural Ireland in contrast to Britain, where there were many shops selling bacon and cheese to rural labourers. He concluded that this was because, in contrast to Britain, where most agricultural labourers were paid a cash wage, in Ireland most labourers had little spending power because their labour income and the money earned from the sale of a pig was absorbed by their rent, and their food consisted almost entirely of the potatoes they produced.

Inglis was shocked by the attitude of even resident landlords towards the management of their estates and their tenants. He encountered 'a wealthy and unembarrassed baronet' who when asked

> why he did not embellish his domain which stood greatly in need of it and thus give some employment to the people, said he made it a rule to circumscribe within the least possible limits his intercourse with the lower orders.[22]

Inglis found most landlords 'extremely ignorant of the real condition of the poor' and pointed out that

> they do not themselves hire labour nor call on the small farmer for rent. They do not themselves eject or drive for rent – and it is not to the hall but to the farmhouse that the mendicant and

the mendicant's wife and the orphan child and the unemployed labourer carry their sack and their petitions.[23]

Another perceptive visitor to Ireland was James Ebenezer Bicheno (1785–1851), an English writer, naturalist and later colonial secretary of van Diemen's Land who would be appointed as one of the poor commissioners. Bicheno published his impressions of the country as *Ireland and its economy* in 1830.[24] He noted how backward Irish agriculture was and considered that Ireland's agricultural system was 'as we know to have prevailed in England in the thirteenth and fourteenth centuries, that is by cottiers, whose capital consisted in their labour, and who paid part or the whole of their rent by working a certain portion of time for their landlord'.[25]

Bicheno saw the incidence of absentee landlords and sub-letting as the major cause of the poverty of the labourers. Bicheno contrasted the situation in England, where most labourers were paid a living wage, and had some security of tenure, with the exploitative rack renting of the Irish landlords. He described Irish landlords as 'needy, exacting, unremitting, harsh and without sympathy for their tenants'.[26] Bicheno perceived that the Irish system of land-letting was not sustainable. He pointed out that Irish landlords, by treating their land 'simply as an article of profit', led 'to methods of letting which are ruinous to the tenant and in the end will be ruinous to himself (the landlord)'.[27] Like Inglis, Bicheno was appalled by the housing of the labourers. He wrote of the labourers' cabins that 'the general aspect of these hovels from a distance is that of heaps of dung reeking with the steam of their own fermentation'.[28]

Bicheno quoted from Arthur Young's account of his visit to Ireland in 1772 to show that the living conditions of labourers had seriously deteriorated between 1772 and 1829. He pointed out that Young had seen no evidence of real hunger among the poorest and had found that they were no poorer than their contemporaries in England and Wales.

The most obvious manifestation of the extent of extreme poverty in Ireland in the early nineteenth century was the ever-increasing number of beggars. Ciarán McCabe in his pioneering study shows how the ubiquity of begging in Ireland drew the attention and concern of social commentators, religious activists and travellers.[29]

Mendicancy and vagrancy (many beggars being also vagrants) were linked to agrarian unrest, as many beggars were evicted tenants, and to disease. Irish poverty, as evidenced by the alarming prevalence of begging, became a political issue on which the British government was pressed to act. Contemporary politicians and other public figures were aware of the ever-increasing numbers of people living in near destitution in Ireland and some Irish MPs at Westminster began to demand government action on poor relief in Ireland.

# 2. Poverty and its relief in Ireland, 1800–38

England had a poor law from 1605 that required Church of England parishes to make minimal provision for the poor in the parish, but the Poor Law Act did not apply in Ireland. Some medical charities provided care for the sick poor but there was no public provision for the old, the disabled or the unemployed, many of whom survived by begging. While there was no statutory provision for the poor in Ireland, Church of Ireland parishes had civil roles that included giving alms to the poor in the form of money, food, fuel and clothes.[1] This relief was funded by the parish 'cess' or locally imposed rate. Parishes also had the power to issue resident beggars with badges with the aim of ensuring that wandering beggars were not assisted by the parish. The parish-based relief system was limited in its scope and was effective mainly in the east and north-east of Ireland where the Church of Ireland had more members and parishes were more prosperous.

In addition to parish-based poor relief, twelve houses of industry were established from 1773 onwards whose function was to be a place of detention and industry for unlicensed beggars.[2] The houses of industry by the early nineteenth century were increasingly admitting the sick poor and thus were unable to solve the problem of street begging, which had increased greatly as a result of the economic depression, distress and dislocation that followed the ending of the Napoleonic Wars in 1815 and the demobilization of large numbers of soldiers. The increase in street begging led to a campaign for the establishment of new organizations to suppress it. In the absence of action by central or local government, groups of professional men and merchants formed Mendicity Societies that raised voluntary funds for the relief of poverty.[3] Between 1809 and 1845, fifty-two Mendicity Institutions were established in Ireland. The paupers served by the mendicity institutions did not in most cases reside in the buildings but were admitted in the morning, provided with food and discharged in the evening when they returned home or slept on the streets. The able-bodied were put to work breaking stones or oyster shells, picking oakum or spinning. Some institutions provided basic education for children.

The increasing numbers living in poverty in rural Ireland contributed to a rise in agrarian violence, with the resurgence of Whiteboys and other violent groups leading to a breakdown in justice in rural Ireland. The British government began to accept that poverty was the cause of this violence and sought ways of reducing it. Another factor bringing the attention of British policy makers to Irish poverty was the flood of impoverished Irish people arriving in Britain after the inauguration of steamships between Dublin and Holyhead in 1816. Though some of those Irish labourers found work on British farms or in factories, many ended up begging on the streets of the cities. McCabe cites estimates that 20 per cent of beggars in London were Irish.[4] The Irish immigrants were also seen as a threat to British labour by driving down wages and as a possible burden on the poor law.

In response to the famine and subsequent typhoid epidemic of 1817, the House of Commons in 1819 established a select committee to investigate both disease and the conditions of the working poor in Ireland.[5] The committee concluded that a recurrence of the typhoid epidemic could be prevented only if the conditions of the people were improved and pauperism and mendicity diminished. The select committee found that, while in response to the epidemic fever hospitals had been built and aid given to the poorest in the form of money and provisions, they had only stemmed the epidemic but had not eliminated typhoid.

Another famine, in 1822, again alerted the British government and public to the endemic poverty in Ireland and the failure of Irish landlords to deal with it. The failure of Irish landlords to make any provision for their impoverished tenants, thereby imposing the burden of relief on English taxpayers, was frequently criticized in the British parliament and was a major driver of the efforts to establish an Irish poor law funded by rates levied on Irish landowners. A Select Committee on the Employment of the Poor in Ireland was established and reported in 1825. Its report attributed increasing poverty in Ireland to subdivision of land, which facilitated rapid population increase leading to higher rents and more evictions which, in turn, caused agrarian violence.[6] The committee reached the significant conclusion that the famine of 1822 stemmed less from the lack of food than from the lack of means to buy it. Parliament passed an Irish Poor Employment Act, which allocated £100,000 for public works, mainly road building, in Ireland. While accepting that chronic unemployment was the major cause of Irish poverty, the committee rejected government provision for the poor and recommended developing Ireland's resources of agriculture and fishing, subsidized emigration and charitable loans associations.

Outbursts of agrarian violence in 1824–5 caused the British parliament to set up a Committee on the State of Ireland in 1825.[7] The committee heard evidence that only one in twenty of Irish labourers was employed and those only occasionally. The excess supply of agricultural labour drove wages to below subsistence level, leaving huge numbers of labourers destitute and needing to beg for part of the year to survive. Though several witnesses heard by the committee recommended a poor law for Ireland, the committee's reports ignored their suggestions and, in its conclusions, emphasized religious strife, tithes, rental practices and the administration of justice as the causes of agrarian violence. Between 1822 and 1830, several poor-law bills were introduced at Westminster with the aim of forcing Irish landed proprietors to support their own poor, and while none got past a first reading, their introduction kept the issue of Irish poverty at the centre of British government concerns.[8]

In response to famine caused by local failures of the potato crop in 1830, mainly in Munster, a parliamentary Committee on the State of the Poor in Ireland was established and charged to 'take into consideration the state of the poorer classes in Ireland and the best means of improving their condition'.[9] The committee heard evidence from many witnesses of the ever-increasing level of poverty in Ireland, with some claiming that one-sixth of the population were dependent on charity. The committee's report recommended nineteen bills to ameliorate poverty in Ireland, the most significant being the establishment of a Board of Works to fund and carry out improvements in roads, bridges, canals, piers and harbours. The committee failed to make a recommendation on whether a poor law should be introduced in Ireland but there were continued demands from both Irish and English MPs for an Irish poor law.

While the necessity of a poor law for Ireland was being debated, opponents of the English poor law, who claimed it was being abused and led to malingering, succeeded in having a poor law enquiry commission established to investigate it in 1832. This commission recommended a radical change from the old poor law, in operation from the early seventeenth century, which provided parish-based relief to the poor, to a much harsher system based on workhouses. Irish politicians and commentators argued that the Irish poor should have the same rights to relief as the poor in England. Some English MPs were concerned about the increasing numbers of Irish immigrants arriving in England seeking employment and, when not finding it, seeking relief under the English poor law, at the expense of English ratepayers. The establishment in 1832 of the Royal Commission on the English poor laws created pressure on the government to take some action on the state of the poor in Ireland, which was very clearly much worse than that of the English poor. Catholic Emancipation in 1829 had enabled the election of Catholics to the parliament of the United Kingdom and the thirty-nine Irish MPs soon sought to influence government policy on Ireland through motions and bills, several of which sought the establishment of an Irish poor law.

The lord lieutenant of Ireland, Lord Anglesey, in March 1833 submitted a plan for an Irish poor law and labour rate, drafted by Richard Griffith, the valuation commissioner, and Anthony Blake, a Dublin Castle official, to the Whig government. Sir Robert Peel, leader of the opposition Conservatives, suggested in April 1833 that an enquiry be held into poverty in Ireland after the forthcoming English poor-law report.

During a debate in Westminster on a proposal for an Irish poor law in May 1833, Lord Althorp, chancellor of the exchequer, while expressing scepticism of the need for an Irish poor law, announced the establishment of an enquiry into poverty in Ireland.[10] That the Whig government intended that any provision for the poor in Ireland be limited is revealed in a letter from Lord Melbourne, the home secretary, to Lord Monteagle, secretary to the treasury, in which he mentioned that the groundwork had been laid for 'the establishment in Ireland of a provision for the old, infirm and infants by the appointment of a commission to enquire into the condition of the poor in Ireland'.[11] There is no mention of the able-bodied poor, who constituted the largest number living in poverty in Ireland. The commission was established in 1833.

# 3. The establishment of a royal commission to enquire into the condition of the poorer classes in Ireland[1]

The government's first choice as chair of the commission was the Tory MP and landlord Thomas Frankland Lewis, who had served on the Irish Revenue Commission of 1820 and who had been a member of the 1817 Sturges Bourne inquiry into poor relief in England. He had strongly supported that commission's recommendation that poor relief be greatly reduced. Lewis, who would chair the English Poor Law Commission of 1834, declined the offer of the chair of the Irish commission but nominated his son, George Cornwall Lewis, who was appointed an ordinary member.

When Lewis refused the chairmanship, it was immediately offered to Richard Whately, Anglican archbishop of Dublin (1787–1863) (fig. 1). Whately, who was born in England, was actively involved in political and economic debates in Ireland and England. Before his appointment as archbishop of Dublin, Whately had been Drummond Professor of Political Economy at Oxford and had established the Chair of Political Economy at Trinity College, which still bears his name. He was known to be sceptical of the feasibility of a poor law for Ireland. Another clergyman hostile to poor laws, Revd William Corrie, a non-practising Unitarian minister from Birmingham, was appointed along with William Battie-Wrightson, a Yorkshire landowner and barrister who had extensive experience of poor-law administration in Doncaster, as paid commissioners. The Irish-based commissioners did not receive any payment. Whately suggested the appointment of Dr Daniel Murray, the Catholic archbishop of Dublin with whom he had worked successfully on the board that had established primary schools in Ireland. Murray was involved in sponsoring considerable charitable work but showed little

1. Archbishop Richard Whately (1787–1863)
by kind permission of the National Portrait Gallery, London

enthusiasm for state support for the poor. Whately also appointed Revd James Carlile, a Presbyterian minister who had also worked with him on the Education Board. Dr Charles Vignoles, chaplain to the lord lieutenant, and Fenton Hort, a Dublin landowner involved in charitable work, were also appointed on Whately's suggestion. Two appointees, Richard More-O'Farrell and James Naper, were intended to appease two different political constituencies in Ireland – the growing Catholic middle class and the Protestant landed gentry. More-O'Farrell, a Catholic Irish landowner, had been an active member of Daniel O'Connell's Irish Association but by 1833 was a Whig-Liberal MP for Co. Kildare while James Naper, a large landowner of Loughcrew in Co. Meath, had submitted a plan for an Irish poor law that had been commented on approvingly in an 1830 Commons debate on Irish poor relief. More-O'Farrell, who took little part in the commission's work during its first year, resigned in 1834, largely because of the commission's failure to intervene in the starvation and disease crisis he witnessed in the west of Ireland in the summer of 1834. He was replaced by another Catholic landlord, Lord Killeen, who was close to the Dublin Castle administration.

Two additional commissioners were appointed at points when the commission's work was stalling. One of those, James Ebenezer Bicheno, had suggested himself as a member when the commission was being established and had been nominated by Lord Lansdowne, lord president of the council for the original commission, but not accepted. When a vacancy occurred, he was again nominated by Lansdowne and accepted. Bicheno regarded himself, with some justification, as an expert on Ireland and on the poor laws and had published an account of his travels in Ireland, cited above, in which he had written that the level of poverty in Ireland was greater than in any of the other European countries he had visited. Bicheno was to be the third paid commissioner in addition to Corrie and Battie-Wrightson. He was hostile to the introduction of an Irish poor law and had campaigned for making the English poor law more restrictive. The second commissioner who was added after the commission was established, Anthony Blake, was chief remembrancer to the exchequer, and was recruited in 1835 when it was proving difficult to distil the large volume of evidence collected into a coherent final report. Blake, a Catholic, was an adviser to all the Dublin Castle administrations between the 1820s and the 1840s and was known to be hostile to poor relief.

The commission appointed as secretary John Revans who had been secretary to the English Poor Law Commission. A team of assistant commissioners was appointed to carry out the enquiries throughout the country. It was decided that both English and Irish assistant commissioners would be appointed as it was considered that English commissioners might not understand the cultural differences between England and Ireland. The assistant commissioners included barristers, army officers, clergymen and government officials. The English assistant commissioners were paid and while the Irish assistant commissioners were not paid, they were given generous expenses.

The composition of the Irish Poor Commission and its recommendations should be viewed in the context of a debate that had been underway during the early years of the nineteenth century on the role of private charity and state provision in the alleviation of poverty. Christian political economists, of whom Whately was an eminent example, tried to reconcile the teachings of natural and revealed theology with the insights of political economy to explain the existence of inequality and poverty in human society and to suggest responses to them. Their principal teaching was that poverty and inequality were ordained by God to stimulate the practice of benevolence, which they considered essential to human progress. For the state to try to force benevolence to the poor through statutory entitlements, or to intervene in the market economy, would violate the principles of both Divine Providence and Political Economy and would ultimately retard human progress.

In a sermon published in 1835,[2] Archbishop Whately noted that Christ frequently healed the sick but on only one occasion fed the hungry, when he performed the miracle of the loaves and fishes. Sickness befalls people through no fault of their own, but hunger could result from their lack of industry or improvidence. Whately believed that what he considered the harmony produced by laissez-faire was evidence of Divine wisdom and that state intervention would be a questioning of that wisdom. Whately and other members of the Poor Law Commission considered that voluntary associations and charities should be encouraged and supported to relieve the suffering of the sick and aged poor and widows and orphans but that no provision should be made for the able-bodied unemployed.

# 4. Social unrest and politics in 1830s Westmeath

When the Poor Commission began its investigations, all the land of Westmeath was owned by a small number of landlords who leased it to tenants. While the Anglo-Norman families of Tuite and Nugent had held onto substantial estates, most of the landlords had obtained their land in the Cromwellian confiscations. George Nugent, marquess of Westmeath, who gave evidence to the Poor Commission, was the lord lieutenant of the county. The landlords rented their land to tenants, many of whom sub-let their farms, with the result that 37 per cent of tenants had between two and twenty acres while 41 per cent had less than one acre.[1] Thirty-eight per cent of houses were fourth-class as defined in the 1841 census, that is one-roomed cabins of stone or mud with at most one window and in many cases without a chimney.[2] The agricultural labourers who lived in those cabins paid the rent for the cabin and potato patch by working for tenant farmers and landlords, or from the sale of a pig. Some were granted conacre in lieu of wages. The conacre land was let to the labourers manured and ready to receive a crop of potatoes and rents were driven up to exorbitant levels due to competition for land. The rapidly increasing population of landless labourers and labourer/farmers, whose only means of subsistence was a patch of land on which to grow potatoes, resulted in fierce competition for available land. The desperate pressure of rapidly increasing population on land in Westmeath is shown by the fact that in the 1830s mud cabins were occupied and potatoes were being cultivated on the Hill of Uisneach, the highest point in the county and the mythical centre of Ireland. The hill still has the outline of parallel ridges about six feet wide which were pejoratively called 'lazy beds' but which were the only way in which potatoes could be grown in rough, stony ground. After the Famine the lazy beds on Uisneach returned to pasture.[3]

Competition for land often led to intimidation and violence in disputes over the letting of land. Secret agrarian societies variously known as Whiteboys, Peep-o'-day-boys, Steel Boys, Thrashers, Righters, Carders and Shanavats had existed from the mid-eighteenth century and their activity resurged as economic conditions deteriorated in the 1820s.[4] G.E. Christianson notes that Westmeath was one of the counties in which those societies had continuously existed from the 1790s to the 1840s.[5] Agrarian violence was seldom directed against the landlords who, being armed and living in well-protected mansions, would not have been easy targets. The violence was usually aimed at the tenant of a piece of land from which another tenant had been evicted or not had his lease renewed. Intimidation and violence were also directed at landlord's agents, bailiffs and process servers and tithe proctors who collected the tithe, or tax on agricultural produce, which Catholics as well as Protestants were obliged to pay to support the Church of Ireland clergy.[6]

The extent of agrarian violence in Westmeath in the 1830s is shown by a schedule of offences committed in the four months since the previous assizes, which the judge at the Westmeath County Assizes of July 1831 had drawn up.[7] The schedule included seventeen houses burned, twenty-two assaults connected to Ribbonism, sixty-eight illegal notices, nine illegal meetings, twenty-one injuries to property and twenty-seven attacks on houses. The judge stated that the term assault in the case of the Ribbonmen attacks was 'very confining', suggesting that the assaults were very brutal. The judge commented that none of those offences was before the court, which indicates that victims of the crimes feared giving evidence in court against the perpetrators. He also thought that there was a high level of unreported crime.[8]

The Poor Commission was established soon after Catholic Emancipation, which resulted in MPs being elected in Westmeath and in other constituencies who would for the first time represent, to some extent, the interests of the Irish poor at Westminster. From 1801 to 1826 the two Westmeath seats at Westminster were held successively by Hercules Pakenham, Gustavus Rochfort and William Smyth and his son Robert Smyth. All were owners of large estates in Westmeath and supported the Tories. As MPs were not paid a salary, only the wealthy, mainly landowners, could afford to stand for parliament. Only those men who owned or leased property with a valuation of 40s. (two British pounds) could vote in elections and voters had to openly declare for whom they were voting. Tenants voted for the landlords for fear of being evicted or having their rent raised. Elections were tumultuous events with candidates plying voters with food and alcohol and, in many cases, simply paying voters to vote for them.

In the General Election of 1826, Daniel O'Connell's Catholic Emancipation movement, which had as its objective the ending of the remaining Penal Laws, particularly the obstacles to Catholics becoming MPs at Westminster, fielded candidates in several constituencies. In Westmeath, Hugh Morgan Tuite of Sonna, described as a 'radical' for his support of Catholic Emancipation, stood for election (fig. 2). He stressed his independence from 'any particular line of politics', his belief that emancipation would restore 'peace and good order' and his wish to deliver the county 'from the degradation of being considered a sort of family property, or hereditary borough'.[9] Tuite was a member of an Anglo-Norman family settled in Westmeath from the twelfth century. His grandfather had converted to Protestantism in the eighteenth century to retain his lands, but the Tuites remained sympathetic to the grievances of Catholics. The Tuites were commended for giving 'perpetual employment to a number of our poor' and spending 'a splendid fortune'.[10] Tuite was elected as the second candidate for Westmeath. The under-secretary for Ireland, Sir William Gregory, in a letter to Sir Robert Peel, the chief secretary, reported that 'Popish priests are endeavouring to detach the tenants from their Protestant landlords in Westmeath to support Tuite, but they are not expected to succeed'.[11] The election involved violent conflict between supporters of the candidates, with two men killed and over one hundred wounded in clashes that 'would disgrace the inhabitants of New Zealand'.[12] On the first day of voting, Tuite arrived in Mullingar in 'a caravan drawn by a motley crew of the *sans culottes* armed with bludgeons'.[13] It was reported that priests were 'very busy about the booths, threatening, persuading and noting down such as voted contrary to their wishes', whom they advised to 'prepare their coffins or leave the country'.[14] While Tuite praised the 'good temper and orderly conduct' of the election and distributed silver coins to his supporters, a mob later went on a rampage shouting 'Come out, you bloody Orangemen' and 'We have not forgotten '98 yet'.[15]

**2.** Sir Hugh Morgan Tuite (1795–1868)

As a result of the unrest and violence attending Tuite's election, a petition was submitted to the House of Commons pleading that he should not be allowed to take his seat.[16] Tuite did not oppose the petition, but his supporters did and a committee of enquiry decided in his favour. He took his seat in time to vote for Catholic relief on 12 May 1828 and for the duke of Wellington's Catholic Emancipation Bill on 6 March 1829. Tuite was defeated in the 1831 election but was re-elected in 1841 and served until 1847. He was appointed to the Board of Guardians of the Poor Law when it was established in 1838. He provided generous Famine relief in Westmeath and resigned from the Board of Guardians of the Poor Law in protest at the 'quarter-acre clause' amendment to the Irish poor law, introduced by Sir William Gregory, which required anybody owning more than a quarter of an acre of land to surrender it to the landlord before they could qualify for poor relief.[17]

While Sir Hugh Morgan Tuite was an example of a resident landlord who took an active interest in the management of his estates and sought to improve the lot of the poor in Westmeath, Sir Francis Hopkins (1813–60), who became the owner of the Rochfort estate near Mullingar in 1837,[18] was an example of the absentee landlords whose lack of direct involvement in managing their estates, and the remittance of much of their rental income from Ireland to England and other European countries, contributed significantly to the under-development of pre-Famine Ireland.

Hopkins was born in Co. Meath and succeeded to his title at the age of 1 in 1814 on the death of his father (fig. 3). In 1834, at the age of 21, he inherited his father's estate and could live in affluence on its substantial rental income without visiting it. Using money inherited from his father, Hopkins bought the Rochfort estate near Mullingar and neighbouring lands, without seeing them, in 1837 and did not visit until February 1838. He walked the estate with his agent on 4 February and distributed alms to some impoverished tenants but on 6 February he recorded in his diary that he had 'some cabins thrown down'.[19] He does not record whether the owners of the cabins were in arrears with their rent or whether the cabins had been built on marginal land without Hopkins's permission. In 1839, two years after buying the Rochfort estate, Hopkins received a threatening letter, which stated that 'if you do not be lighter on your tenants than what you are, you shall be surely shot'.[20] This threat was almost certainly issued by the Ribbonmen, a secret society defending the interests of tenants, which was active in Westmeath in the 1830s.[21] Four murders of landowners in Westmeath in 1838 and 1839 were attributed to Ribbonmen. Such was the level of agrarian violence in Westmeath in the late 1830s that a group of Westmeath landlords petitioned the lord lieutenant to order a 'general and simultaneous search' for firearms. In April 1839 a committee of the House of Lords enquired into the 'state of Ireland in respect to Crime and Outrage'.[22] Sir Francis Hopkins's evidence to this committee may explain why he received a death threat. He stated that on taking possession of the Rochfort estate many tenants were in arrears of rent and that he had instructed his agent to collect the rents as soon as they were due and to make three months after they were due the date by which they must be collected. Tenants had previously been allowed six months after the

**3.** Sir Francis Hopkins (1813–61)

due date to pay rents. Hopkins stated that after issuing this notice a representative of his tenants had informed him that they thought he wished to get rid of tenants by demanding that they pay up their rents, which they were not able to do. Hopkins stated that he had not succeeded in collecting rents as he wished but that he had not issued any notices to quit. Hopkins's assertion that he had not evicted tenants is contradicted by evidence that several tenants had been evicted after the partial failure of the potato crop in 1836 and more would be evicted after further crop failures in 1839, 1841 and 1843.[23]

A tenant evicted after the 1843 partial potato-crop failure, Brian Seery, would in 1846 be convicted of attempting to murder Hopkins. Hopkins evicted Seery because he believed Seery did not have enough capital to effectively farm the forty acres he rented. Seamus O'Brien argues that Seery's eviction was evidence that Hopkins, like other landlords of his time, was attempting to consolidate smaller farms into larger, more viable units. Hopkins believed that his eviction of Seery was the motive for Seery's attempt on his life. That landlords felt insecure after the partial failure of the potato crop in 1843 and the growing unrest among tenants, who would have sympathized with Seery, is indicated by the fact that a special commission rather than the regular assizes was requested by the landlords to try Seery. Seery's first trial collapsed because two Catholic jurors refused to find him guilty. A second trial was held with a jury entirely composed of Protestants, which convicted Seery who was sentenced to death. Though Seery swore on the gallows that he was innocent, Patrick Casey believes that he was guilty.[24]

Hopkins made extensive improvements to Rochfort House but between 1837 and 1846 he spent very little time there, preferring to live in London and travel extensively. He left the management of the estate largely to his agents. On his visits to his estate, Hopkins did take some interest in improvements and changed his agents several times. When a poor law was introduced in Ireland in 1838, Hopkins was appointed to the board of guardians but, in contrast to Hugh Morgan Tuite who resigned from the board in protest at the 'quarter-acre clause', Hopkins sought to make the lives of the paupers in the workhouse more wretched. The *Westmeath Guardian* reported in 1844 that the average cost of a pauper was 1s. 3d. 'under the late changes in dietary introduced by Sir Francis Hopkins, Bart., which had reduced the cost from 1s. 6d.'[25] Memories of Hopkins recorded in the Schools Collection of folklore gathered in 1937 record that he 'was not a bad man, but his agents were always telling him lies about the tenants of the estate, and doing all in their power to get them evicted'.[26]

Given the misery of their lives, it is not surprising that many poor people in 1830s Westmeath drank heavily. Whiskey was cheap and the countryside abounded in public houses and illegal distilleries. Fair days were occasions of drinking and fighting. At the May fair of 1831 in Castlepollard, drunken fights broke out around a show tent.[27] The constabulary tried to clear the fair green by confronting the rioting crowd with fixed bayonets, but the crowd did not retreat and threw volleys of stones at the police who retreated to the market house. The chief constable read the Riot Act, but the stone-throwing continued and the chief constable ordered his men to fire. The firing continued for eight to ten minutes and thirteen people were killed and many injured, though how many was not enumerated. At the July assizes of 1831, eighteen policemen were tried for manslaughter and were acquitted by a jury of the Protestant gentry of Westmeath, despite evidence that the police had continued to fire for eight to ten minutes after the crowd had run for their lives.

Such was the extent of agrarian violence in Westmeath in 1831 that a notice was posted in the *Westmeath Journal* seeking a meeting of 'the county', by which was meant the aristocracy and gentry, to consider the disturbed state of the county and to adopt measures to deal with lawlessness.[28] The notice was signed by twenty-seven gentlemen including nine members of the grand jury.

Law and order in Westmeath were enforced by the Royal Irish Constabulary, a full-time professional police force that had been established in 1822 by Sir Robert Peel, chief secretary for Ireland. They were commonly called 'Peelers'. In Westmeath, the force had eight chief constables, sixty-four constables, and 178 sub-constables. The force was distributed in fifty-three barracks located throughout the county. John Kenny points out that many of the barracks were located close to the gates of the demesnes of the gentry, which indicated how insecure the gentry felt at a time of agrarian unrest.[29] The extent of this unrest was outlined by George Nugent, marquess of Westmeath, in evidence to a select committee of the UK parliament in 1823.[30] The marquess stated that Co. Westmeath was in a disturbed state 'principally due to the alienation of the mass of the people, as to their affections, from the state … and from the existing government of the country'.[31] The marquess attributed much of the unrest to the 'superabundant population', the subdivision of land and the oppression of tenants by middlemen. He acknowledged that there were hundreds of people living in misery on his estates in Westmeath and Roscommon. The marquess pointed out that the laws relating to land title were arcane and favoured middlemen to such an extent that some landlords had little involvement in the management of their estates. He claimed that he did not have accurate information on even the names of his own tenants or the rent they were paying. The marquess also condemned the phenomenon of 'forty-shilling freeholders', claiming that some landlords created them by leasing worthless land to paupers in order to create voters who would be obliged to vote for them in elections to parliament.[32]

# 5. The Poor Commission's investigations in Westmeath[1]

The commission began its work by sending out questionnaires on the living conditions of the poor to 7,600 local notables throughout Ireland, including Catholic and Protestant clergymen, dispensary doctors, magistrates and landlords. Some 3,100 replies were received covering 1,100 parishes, a response rate of 47 per cent, which would be regarded as a very good rate today. Based on the answers to the questionnaires, handbooks were written to guide the oral enquiries. In taking oral evidence, it was decided to choose several parishes, roughly one for each barony, in each of the seventeen counties in which oral enquiries would be held. The parishes chosen for investigation in Westmeath were Ballynacargy and Kilbixy, Benowen, Castletown Delvin, Castlepollard, Killucan, Moate and Multyfarnham.[2]

The commission identified seven groups of poor people whose circumstances they would investigate. These were: deserted and orphan children, illegitimate children and their mothers, widows having families of young children, the impotent through age or other permanent infirmity, the sick poor who, in health, would be capable of earning their subsistence, the able-bodied out of work and those who resorted to 'vagrancy as a means of relief'.

For each parish investigated, a group of parishioners, representative of the social groups in the parish, was chosen and included a member of the landed gentry, the Catholic parish priest or curate, the Protestant rector, a farmer, a business proprietor, a labourer and, in some areas, one or more beggars (fig. 4). In Westmeath, the people who gave evidence on the extent of poverty in their parish included the marquess of Westmeath and 'Peggy Kiernan, a beggar with three children, her husband begging with three more in another part of the country'.[3]

Although the able-bodied unemployed constituted the largest proportion of the poor, the questionnaires did not ask respondents

**BEGGAR-WOMAN AND CHILDREN.**

4. Beggar woman and children from 'Ireland and the Irish'
(*Illustrated London News*, 12 Aug. 1843)

to estimate the number of able-bodied people out of work in their
parish but asked them to estimate the extent of labour migration. In
most parishes the answer to how many labourers left the parish to seek
work elsewhere was 'none', 'a few' or '10 to 20' but in some parishes,
migration was substantial. In Drumraney, Revd P. Malinn, parish
priest, stated that about one hundred left to seek work with about
thirty going to England. In Clonard, the parish priest, Revd Michael

Berry, stated that one hundred labourers migrated, mostly to England, while in Killucan Revd John Curran, the parish priest, thought about two hundred left to seek seasonal work. In Castlepollard, W. Pollard JP (Justice of the Peace) stated that few labourers in his parish migrated to England, but many went to Meath to harvest wheat or to Kildare to harvest potatoes.

In the parish of Mayne, Gerard Dease JP stated that about thirty labourers migrated from his parish to Meath or Dublin for work on the harvest, but none went to England. In Castletown Delvin, Revd P. Fitzgerald thought that about three hundred labourers migrated, mainly to neighbouring counties for work on the harvest. In Mullingar, Revd Alex Gibson, Presbyterian Minister, stated that not many labourers left his parish because 'they are anticipated by their poorer Connaught brethren'.[4] He stated that, of those who went to England, few returned. Revd John Kearney, parish priest of Kilkenny West, stated that while about sixty labourers left his parish for harvest work in neighbouring counties, few went to England 'on account of the maltreatment they were threatened with by English labourers'.

Respondents were asked how the wives and children of migrant labourers survived in their absence. Some responded that married men in their parish did not migrate. The wives and children of the married men who did migrate survived on their store of potatoes or on provisions their husbands left for them.[5] Some women and children were employed on farms while others got credit until their husband returned. In Drumraney the priest reported that the wives and children of migrant workers 'laboured under many privations. Many were reduced to begging'.[6] The cynical J. Lyons JP from Mullingar responded 'I know nothing about the wives but there is a great deal of diversity of colour in the hair of the children',[7] which suggested that the wives of the migrant labourers might not have been faithful to their absent husbands.

In the oral hearings there was some disagreement among witnesses as to how long labourers were out of work during the year. In Multyfarnham, Mr Young, the Protestant curate, thought half the labourers were unemployed for six months while George Gibson, a farmer, thought two months and Revd James Dowling, the Catholic parish priest, said three months. Most witnesses agreed that most labourers were unemployed for most of the period from November to March and in June and July. This was because most labourers were casual workers, employed only during the sowing and harvesting seasons, rather than full-time workers. During the period November to March, the labourers usually had enough potatoes to eat but by June most had exhausted their stock of potatoes. A witness in Ballynacargy/Kilbixy stated that labourers often had to resort to digging immature potatoes in June and July, which not only had little nutritional value, but reduced the final crop yield and the stock for the ensuing winter.

Mr John Monveal, a miller, who gave evidence in Benowen, showed a detailed knowledge of the economic conditions of labourers. He stated that most labourers had only one rood of ground for which they paid £2 15s. in rent. This area of land would produce about nine barrels of potatoes, but each family would consume three stone of potatoes per day, which meant that the total output of potatoes would feed the family until about 1 April when the labourer would be employed. The refuse of the potatoes with about 5s. worth of bran would fatten a pig, which would cost the labourer 6s. and sell for £2. The profit on the sale of the pig was therefore less than the rent of the potato patch and the labourer still had to find £1 for the rent of his cabin.

During the summer months, the labourer would be employed at 8d. per day on average. But the labourer must now buy potatoes from his earnings and during the summer months the price of potatoes on average was 3½d. per stone and could rise to 10½d. per stone. The labourer would therefore have to spend 10½d. per day on potatoes while earning at most 6d. per day. The labourer's earnings were therefore inadequate to feed his family, much less cover the rent of his cabin. Given this situation, Monveal stated that most labourers were obliged to reduce their consumption of potatoes to one stone per day, supplemented with cabbage or weeds. Monveal stated that he had visited labourers' houses and had seen 'children crying; the father was there, but had nothing to give them, and could get no work'.[8]

Given the situation described by Monveal, it is not surprising that many witnesses stated that labourers' wives and children were driven to begging during the summer and in some cases the labourers had to borrow money at extortionate interest rates. In Castletown Delvin, Mr Hope, a farmer, stated that labourers sometimes obtained provision on credit and that the price charged was 'generally about a fourth more than the money price at the time the credit was given'.[9] Hope thought that credit was becoming harder to access and that this was 'one reason of the increase in vagrancy'.[10] In Killucan, Matthew Keeffe, a farmer, stated that provisions were given on credit to labourers 'at a price materially above the rate of the market'.[11] Keeffe stated that 'this system is very injurious to the labourer, but he cannot do without it'.[12] In Ballynacargy/Kilbixy a witness stated that out-of-work labourers got credit from farmers as otherwise they would starve. The witness stated that the system of credit 'had a strong tendency to keep the labourer in debt and difficulty, which not infrequently produces recklessness and misery, as it would be impossible for a man to lay up any provision against the time of non-employment'.[13]

Some landlords and farmers employed more labourers than they needed, to save them from starvation. In Moate, Hugh Lanigan, a farmer, stated that 'in some seasons men often entreat to be allowed to work for their food alone'.[14] Lanigan noted that while he could get workers to save his harvest for food alone, he 'was ashamed to give them less than 5d. a day and their support'.[15] In Multyfarnham, witnesses stated that 'at seasons of particular distress' farmers and gentlemen employed more labourers than they required. It was stated that in Multyfarnham, on one occasion, when this course was adopted by the influence of Revd Charles Browne, a Church of Ireland clergyman, 'distress was entirely banished thereby'.[16] In Castletown Delvin, Lord Westmeath asserted that Mr Fetherston, lately deceased, had employed more labourers than he required and that 'his death, therefore would cause an irreparable loss'.[17] The Fetherston or Fetherstonhaugh family were large landowners in Delvin.

The only non-farming work available to most labourers would have been on road construction. This work was paid for mainly in food as John Bracken, a road contractor who gave evidence in Mullingar, explained. Bracken stated that he was paid only three times a year when the work was completed and that he had to buy meal on credit at 3s. per cwt above the market price. This additional price was passed on to the men resulting in them getting less meal than if Bracken had not had to buy it on credit.

Several witnesses stated that when they were unemployed, some labourers resorted to crime to be imprisoned or transported. In

Ballynacargy/Kilbixy, Sir Hugh Morgan Tuite stated that while there was no direct evidence that people had committed crimes in the hope of being sent to prison for food and shelter, he could 'in no other way account for the great increase in petty crime'.[18] That hunger drove some labourers to crime was confirmed by Mr West, a magistrate who stated that 'a man under sentence of transportation for an attack on a poor woman's house stated to me that he was induced to the act by information he received that there was a large quantity of meal in the house, he being in absolute want'.[19]

In Mullingar, George Reeves, a shopkeeper, stated that he knew a man 'who used go into the country to cut sticks by the way, in order that he may be put into gaol'.[20] The assistant commissioners decided to investigate the question of whether poverty drove people to commit crimes in the hope of being put in gaol and visited the county gaol in Mullingar where the governor, Mr Fielding, gave them the names of twenty-five mostly young people and of both sexes who had within the previous year committed minor offences 'chiefly, as he believed, to obtain food and shelter of the prison'.[21] The governor said that when 'the plenty, cleanliness and comfort of the gaol' was contrasted with the 'wretchedness of the cabins' it was not surprising that people committed crimes in the hope of being jailed. A witness in Castletown Delvin thought that some people committed robberies 'to relieve themselves of destitution, and some cases are known to enable them to emigrate to America'.[22] This witness thought that such crimes were 'not generally committed by those most in want'.

All witnesses agreed that labourers could not save any money to survive the periods when they were unemployed. In Ballynacargy/Kilbixy the labourers who gave evidence, Patrick Murtagh and William Cox, said 'A labourer thinks he has made sufficient provision for his old age when he has reared up a family. This formerly answered well enough, but now the young men, as soon as they grow up, go off to Australia and leave the old to beg'.[23]

The fact that labourers married early and had large families was noted disapprovingly by Lord Westmeath who made a lengthy comment on this in Castletown Delvin.[24] He believed that the poorest were more likely to make improvident marriages because 'they cannot be worse'.[25] Those with a little property were 'more cautious in marrying than the poor'.[26] Lord Westmeath attributed 'the improvident marriages in Ireland to the habitual interference of the priests in the temporal affairs of the Roman Catholic population'.[27] Lord Westmeath was clearly aware of the population explosion occurring in the 1830s in Ireland. He remarked 'whether an exuberant population are to be employed or to languish, to live or starve, the priests consider numbers as their boast and pride and the source of their newly assumed political power'.[28] The 'newly assumed political power' is a reference to Catholic Emancipation which had occurred in 1829 and which removed the remaining restrictions on the activities of Catholic priests.

In Mullingar Revd Joseph Gibson, a Presbyterian clergyman, also commented on the improvident marriages of labourers. He stated that 'those who have nothing are by far the least cautious in taking on themselves the burthen of a family; they often marry and have not 6*d*. the next morning; and the answer to any remonstrance invariably is "We cannot be worse"'.[29]

The most harrowing evidence of the poverty suffered by unemployed workers came, surprisingly, not from farm labourers but from a weaver and a cooper. In Moate, Robert Kennedy, described as 'formerly a weaver', stated that three years previously

> I was very glad to work 12 weeks at 6*d*. a day without food; I had a wife and child, I got one day a single potato, which I brought home to my child to keep it from starving. I was at one time hard at work and 48 hours without food, except one potato, and I tried to kill the hunger with water.[30]

Kennedy's wife had begged from Revd Mr Rolleston, the Protestant rector, who had given her 2*s*. 6*d*. with which she bought her husband food, but he stated that he could not eat it because his stomach had 'closed up against it'.[31] Kennedy presumably had to resort to agricultural labour because his skills as a hand weaver had been made redundant by the recent introduction of the power loom. A case of a weaver's family in England, who had starved to death when he became unemployed, is cited in the third report of the commission.[32]

James Doherty, a cooper, also gave evidence of the extreme hardship he and his family suffered due to the seasonality of the demand for his skills. He stated that as his main work was making firkins for butter, he was largely unemployed from October to May. He had five children and 'they very seldom get enough to eat, but we are satisfied with whatever we can get'.[33] This remark astonished the assistant commissioners who noted that the quantity of food he considered adequate to feed his family was 'a sum much less than they could conceive to be sufficient'.[34] The assistant commissioners concluded that Doherty did not know how much food his family required to be adequately nourished and that 'through long habit' was as he himself said 'satisfied with whatever he could get'.[35] The assistant commissioners quoted 'a respectable individual well acquainted with the habits of the lower classes' who informed them that they should not 'consider the people here insufficiently well fed, because they consume less food than those of the same rank in England; the fact is that they are accustomed to require less'.[36] These remarks suggest that many labourers and their families were permanently malnourished.

Doherty stated that when he was unemployed, he and his family had only one meal each day and that they would not have survived had not his mother-in-law, who was 'old and not ashamed to do so', gone begging. He went on to describe his poverty further:

> I have not a second shirt and have had this coat these five years and do not know how to get another. I got some weaving to do last winter, but on New Year's Day got sick. Spitting blood; it was brought on by perspiring at my work and getting cold in my cold house. I lost the work as I was three months sick; it would have continued for six months. There is nothing doing now in that way. I was supported in my illness by mother-in-law begging and got nothing to do in my trade since. Dr Middleton told me I could be very well if I had proper food; the last I had was a potato and a bit of salt herring.[37]

The second largest group living in poverty was likely to be those unable to work due to old age or to sickness. Respondents to the questionnaires reported that there were people unable to work due to old age in all parishes. They were mainly supported by their families though in some cases by the 'parish poor money'.[38] In Moylisker, Revd James Meade stated that the old used to be supported by the parish cess 'until it was refused', another reference to the Tithe War.[39] In the parish of Clonard, the Catholic parish priest reported 200 old people incapable of working, all of whom he believed survived by begging. In Killucan, the Catholic parish priest estimated that there were 160 old people supported by 'the farmers in charity'.[40] In Kilbeggan, Revd Edward Wilson stated that a local landlord, Gustavus Lambart, provided pensions for some old people (probably former workers on his estate) but that no other landlords provided such support. Some older people reared poultry and sold eggs or worked for farmers at lighter tasks. Revd William Peacocke, Protestant minister in Drumraney, was concerned that a poor law would 'burst the endearing link between father and son and what the son would have given the father will invariably be spent on whiskey'.[41] In the parish of Clonmellon, the parish priest Revd James Murray stated that a local landlord, Sir James Chapman, had built ten slated houses with five roods of land attached to each for ten 'decayed labourers' on his estate.

At the public hearings witnesses were asked the age at which people in their parish became incapable of supporting themselves and most witnesses agreed that this was around 60, though some people could become incapable of working at 50 because, as a witness in Castletown Delvin stated, 'many become infirm at 50 from exposure to wet, insufficient clothing and other privations'.[42] A witness in Castlepollard also stated that after the age of 50 'they break very fast from the want of proper nourishment'.[43] The witnesses were asked to estimate the number of old people unable to support themselves in their parish. Witnesses in Benowen said about 80 and witnesses in Castletown Delvin about 50. In Castlepollard the witnesses said that the number of those impotent through age was 'very great'.[44] In Killucan the parish priest, Fr Curran, thought there were 400 old people, of whom 300 relied on begging to support themselves, but a local landlord, Mr Purdon, thought there were only seventy, most of whom were supported by their relatives.

Most witnesses agreed that the children or other relatives of the elders supported them and 'the burthen was borne with great willingness' according to a witness in Moate. Witnesses in Multyfarnham stated that children often 'must submit themselves to privation' to support their parents. In some cases, elderly parents moved between their children's homes in order not to be too burdensome to any one of them. In Ballynacargy/Kilbixy, a witness stated that 'the old people are usually worth their keeping, being useful to mind the house and children'.

A less sanguine view of the burden of supporting the elderly was voiced by Pat Geraghty and Philip Lennon, both farmers, who gave evidence in Benowen. They stated that the support of an elderly father-in-law often led to ill feeling: 'his daughter-in-law first begins to dislike the old man; he is at every turn taunted, coming in and going out, till at length he sees clearly he is in the way and takes to the roads as the last resource'.[45] The aged poor who had no relations to care for them were fed by neighbours for a while after they became distressed but 'when the neighbours get tired of them, they are obliged to go through the country to seek alms'.

In Benowen, Michael Finney, described as a beggar, aged 69, gave a first-hand account of how he became a beggar. Having rented four acres of mountain land, he gave it over to his son when he had become 'old and weak and could not work hard enough'.[46] The son could till an acre but 'cannot get manure for more'.[47] The son's winter stock of potatoes was often out before the new crop could be harvested and 'he must stint himself then and use weeds'.[48] The son worked for a while every year in England and while he was away his wife 'keeps five in the house and eats potatoes and salt'.[49] Finney stated that he chose to beg rather than be a burden to his son. He stated 'I am much better off than if I lived with him; I get plenty of potatoes, some milk and even some meat', adding that he was never hungry when begging though he sometimes had been when he lived with his son. Finney stated that he never begged in his local area, as he would be ashamed to do so. He also considered begging better than 'putting a neighbour's duck or goose in the pot'.

The view that the elderly who begged might fare better than those supported by their families was echoed by witnesses in Ballynacargy/ Kilbixy who stated that 'those who do beg are not considered nearly as badly off as many poor householders who are ashamed to do so'.[50] In Benowen, witnesses stated that 'beggars who go out seeking alms are better off, in point of food, than the infirm poor who are living with their relations, though the latter are better taken care of'.

Some older people were supported by remittances from relatives who had emigrated. In Benowen, witnesses stated that 'a good deal of money' was remitted and in Killucan witnesses believed that money was 'frequently sent from America to the friends (i.e., relatives) of persons who have emigrated'.[51] In Moate, Cuthbert Clibborn, a landlord, stated that he had received a remittance of the substantial sum of £8 from America, presumably to pass on to one of his tenants. Presbyterian clergyman Gibson in Mullingar stated that he knew of three persons working in a coal mine in Scotland who sent money home to their relations. Mr Gibson's evidence showed that destitution among the elderly was not confined to the Catholic population as he stated that one of his congregation had 'died in very great distress' and that 'a Catholic beggar woman had supported her for three years by begging through the country'.

Even though some older people who begged seemed to fare better than those supported by their families, most witnesses agreed that 'nothing but extreme want will induce such persons to beg' and that 'mendicancy is always considered as a last resort'.[52]

On the question of organized provision for the old, it was stated that in most parishes this was extremely limited or non-existent. In Ballynacargy, witnesses stated that, while there was no regular contribution fund, the gentry 'behave very generously to the poor' except for absentees 'who contribute nothing'.[53] In Benowen, 'the money collected at places of public worship was given to the most destitute in the parish without any religious distinction' while in Castletown Delvin, congregational collections were given to 'the most indigent' of whom there were about twenty. In Castlepollard, the witnesses stated that 'none are assisted but Protestant widows and sometimes old men'.[54] The amount given to everyone deemed worthy of assistance was two guineas per annum. In Castlepollard, there was 'no subscription made by the gentry for the support of the aged and infirm, or for any class, except rarely and in seasons of particular distress'. In Moate, it was stated that 'in cases of temporary and peculiar distress the gentry subscribe'.[55] Within the previous two years, 'upwards of 750 people were relieved from a fund of this description' and one of the witnesses, Joseph Morton Daly, a landlord, had given away fifteen tons of meal. The behaviour of absentee landlords was commented on in Moate, where witnesses stated that 'absentees living abroad seldom give anything'.[56]

Witnesses in all parishes agreed that given their meagre wages it would be impossible to 'lay up in youth a provision for age', but witnesses in Benowen thought that if labourers received adequate wages such provision would not be necessary as they could support their aged parents, most being willing to do so.

There was considerable disagreement on the issue of a formal provision, funded by taxation, for the old who were unable to work. In Benowen, the witnesses thought that the majority would not accede to a compulsory tax to support the aged 'lest in time it become more extensive'.[57] In Castlepollard, however, witnesses thought that 'if it was properly explained to the people of the parish, the opinion would be most favourable to a provision for the aged poor'.[58] In Killucan, Mr Drought, a magistrate, thought that 'in general the principle of such a provision was approved of, but that it was dreaded; great evils may spring from it'.[59] In the town of Mullingar, witnesses thought that the 'general opinion of the parish was in favour of a provision for the aged poor'.[60] In Multyfarnham, Sir Percy Nugent, a large landlord, and Fr Dowling, the Catholic parish priest, were in favour of a provision for the destitute, but James Flanagan, a farmer, thought the destitute 'were pretty well supported already'.[61] There were no alms-houses for the old in Westmeath. (By the 1830s, many parishes in England had alms-houses.[62])

The poor in early nineteenth-century Ireland were particularly susceptible to the many infectious diseases that were prevalent at the time and for which there was no effective treatment. As many witnesses testified, being unemployed through illness pushed the poor further into poverty as there was little or no support available to the sick poor. A witness in Ballynacargy/Kilbixy stated that it would be 'impossible at the present state of wages for a labourer to lay up any provision against sickness'.[63] In Benowen, John Monveal, the miller, again showed his knowledge of local economic conditions when he stated that even 'a farmer with less than 10 acres, at moderate rent could not provide for a time of sickness'.[64] In Mullingar, the witnesses confirmed Monveal's assertion, stating that 'a labourer never can lay by to provide against a time of sickness and the cottier scarcely ever'.

In times of sickness, the labourers therefore depended mainly on the support of their families and neighbours and on private charity. In Castletown Delvin, witnesses stated that 'the poor are often cautious in attending the sick of contagious diseases, except in cases of relations where they never feel any hesitation'.[65] In Castlepollard, the witnesses agreed that there was 'not much reluctance amongst the poor to attend those sick of contagious diseases'.[66] In Ballynacargy/ Kilbixy, witnesses stated that many poor people were slow to recover from 'fevers and agues' because their families could not provide them with nutritious food. The local doctor, Dr Cotter, stated that a patient of his had had a fever for six weeks and that the medicine he had been given was 'quite useless', but that if the man could have 'beef for dinner and a glass of porter every day, he would soon be at his work again'.

In Moate, Patrick Mulvaney, a labourer, gave a harrowing account of his experience of being out of work through sickness. He said that while he was sick, he was obliged to sell his pig and when the money received for the pig ran out, he and his family lived on eight quarts of meal per week while forty-two quarts would have been barely enough to support his family. He said: 'all the time I was sick we had but one meal a day and two or three times a week we had nothing but weeds.'[67] The assistant commissioners noted that Mulvaney was 'emaciated to a frightful degree and his face was greenish yellow' which the farmers said was invariably the consequence of living on 'prassagh' or wild mustard. Mulvaney explained that he would not be permitted to dig his half-rood of potatoes as he could not pay the rent and the owner of the land had distrained the potato crop. Mr Lanigan, a farmer, commented that he was surprised that Mulvaney had told of his poverty publicly because 'his creditors will be certain to seize all his things and sell them'.[68] Lanigan added that 'you would have many more such miserable stories, if the people were not afraid to have their poverty known'.

In some parishes private charity was available to the sick poor. In Ballynacargy/Kilbixy, there was 'a loan fund of small capital, got up by private subscription and managed by a lady'.[69] Loans of £5 were given, which were paid back in instalments, and losses were rare. In Moate, there was also a loan fund 'supported almost exclusively by a lady and her family'.[70] Loans of £1 to £5 were given and no losses had occurred. In Mullingar, witnesses stated that 'in times of particular distress and when the price of potatoes is above the people's means, a voluntary subscription is entered into and meal and potatoes are sold at about half the market price to those who can pay; to others for less, and to some few, given for nothing'.[71]

In the other parishes there was no fund for assisting the sick poor, but many witnesses felt such a fund was desirable. In Benowen, the Catholic parish priest, Fr Kearney, considered that there would not be 'any danger of encouraging idleness or improvidence' if food or fuel were given to the sick poor, provided their illness was certified by the dispensary doctor, and the fund was administered by the clergy. In Mullingar, the witnesses thought that providing support for the sick poor would be 'most salutary, while the want of it is the cause of recklessness and ruin to the labourer'.[72] In a lengthy intervention in Castletown Delvin, Lord Westmeath expressed his view that 'the excess of pauperism in this agricultural country was owing completely to the injurious subdivision of land in all its modes and manners'.[73] He asked the commission to consider whether, until the subdivision of land was controlled, 'one shilling can be compulsorily laid as a tax upon the country'.[74] Lord Westmeath considered that in a country where 'beyond all example, pauperism is pressing upon property and upon the successful results of industry, the relief of pauperism must be left to spontaneous charity'.[75] Lord Westmeath also attributed the prevalence of pauperism to the resistance of the labourers to agricultural improvement. He stated that 'religious as well as political prejudices operated so strongly to thwart the wishes of proprietors to better modes of cultivation that the Irish poor can rarely lay by anything'.[76] He added that if 'a scientific steward is brought from England or Scotland he is often harassed, injured and driven away'.

Sir Percy Nugent, a landlord and relative of Lord Westmeath, giving evidence in Multyfarnham, was less harsh and thought that giving the sick poor food would not encourage idleness but giving fuel might as it was 'so plenty in this district, that it would be impossible to ascertain whether they possessed any'.[77] Nugent probably had in mind the abundance of bogs in Westmeath on which the labourers would have had rights to harvest turf.

Widows and orphans, single mothers and their children and deserted children were likely to experience poverty and the plight of those groups was examined in each parish. There were widows and orphans in most parishes. In Ballynacargy/Kilbixy the estimate was 'about 20'[78] and in Castletown Delvin 'from 15 to 20'.[79] In Killucan, the estimate was 58 and in Moate there were 'several' but 'taken as a class not numerous'.[80] The widows were supported by their own labour of knitting and spinning, by relatives, by begging or by working for farmers. In the parish of Churchtown, Charles Kelly JP stated that widows in the parish were supported 'by the parish church and other means'.[81] In the parish of Kilbixy, James West JP stated that widows and orphans were supported 'by the resident gentry', while in the neighbouring parish of Rathaspeck and Russagh, Revd James Reynolds PP stated that thirty-four widows and their children were supported by 'their charitable neighbours'.[82] In the small parish of Moylisker, the solitary (and presumably Protestant) widow supported herself by working as sextoness at the Church of Ireland church.

Most witnesses agreed that the widows were very poor but in Benowen, Peggy Kiernan, a beggar, stated that widows worked for farmers in summer and in winter at spinning for which they earned $1\frac{1}{2}d$. per day. Kiernan believed that widows got 'a good deal of private charity, potatoes, milk, meal and all kinds of food'.[83] In contrast to Kiernan's evidence, other witnesses stated that most widows fared very badly with most being able to afford only two meals of potatoes per day with 'not very often a little skimmed milk or buttermilk'.[84] In Castletown Delvin, the witnesses thought that widows fared worse even than beggars and in July and August (before the potato harvest) were reduced to eating 'weeds gathered in the fields'.[85] Witnesses in all parishes stated that widows were often driven to begging and 'sometimes, but very seldom, to prostitution'.[86] The widows, from feelings of shame, usually left the parish to beg, but in Castletown Delvin Mr Hope, a farmer, thought this feeling was subsiding.

Witnesses in some parishes mentioned that widows were sometimes helped from congregational collections but there was 'no general subscription except at times of scarcity'.[87] Lord Westmeath stated that in Castletown Delvin, where he lived, there had been no attempts to 'increase the weekly stipend to the poor with a view to making proselytes'.[88] In Castlepollard, the witnesses stated that seventeen widows were being 'relieved by congregational collections but it is the custom to confine the relief to Protestants'.[89]

Several witnesses stated that labourers who were the neighbours of widows often helped them by giving them a day's or a Sunday morning's labour. In Benowen, the witnesses stated that widows 'could not possibly exist without these private helps from the neighbours.[90] The neighbours also sometimes took charge of one of the widow's children 'if it can be rendered in any way serviceable to them'.

Lord Westmeath stated that a few landlords made some provision for widows of men who had lived and worked on their land, though absentee landlords never made such provision. Mr Hope agreed with Lord Westmeath that some widows were granted cabins and gardens by landowners but stated that even those widows were often reduced to begging as the grant seldom continued throughout the life of the widow. Lord Westmeath explained that 'the state of the law is such a burlesque on common sense that, if, from charity, the landowner allows this to go on too long, it frequently becomes a motive with the pauper to set up a claim of ownership with the proprietor'.[91]

Witnesses in Castletown Delvin stated that widows with children were in general not better off, and often worse off than mothers of illegitimate children, who 'are frequently assisted by the fathers'.[92] This assertion contradicts the evidence of the other witnesses, who stated that the fathers of illegitimate children rarely supported them. In Benowen, the witnesses believed the mothers of illegitimate children fared better than widows because they, 'having less shame, take more readily to begging than widows; and in that way are much better off, as far as regards food'.

In Multyfarnham, witnesses stated that some widows could earn 4*d.* per day by spinning for ten months of the year but that 'no woman with children, however hardworking, could maintain them without some assistance. The Multyfarnham witnesses stated that widows were 'frequently driven to the sale of illicit spirits'.[93] All witnesses agreed that it would be impossible for a labourer, however hard-working or provident, to make any provision for his widow and children in the event of his death.

Respondents to the questionnaires stated that there were few single mothers with children in most parishes but that most of them experienced extreme poverty. Despite their poverty, single mothers very rarely deserted their children. This was confirmed by the answers to the questionnaires which showed that in most parishes there were no deserted children. Only one case of infanticide was recorded by Revd John Young in Multyfarnham, who stated that 'a male child of a few weeks old was found in a bog-hole, drowned, on the estate of Sir Percy Nugent of Donore'.[94] In most parishes where deserted children were recorded, there were only a few and all but one parish stated that no deserted child had perished from neglect. In Mullingar, however, Revd Alex Gibson, the Presbyterian minister, stated that he was 'certain that deserted children had perished from neglect'.[95] The deserted children were supported 'by church contribution', by 'private contributions' or by 'the charity of neighbours'.[96] In the parish of Castlepollard, W.D. Pollard JP reported that the one deserted child in the parish was supported by 'a grant of five shillings from the county'.[97] In some cases, the Church of Ireland clergyman mentioned the children being supported by the 'church cess'.[98] The cess was a tax, like tithes, imposed on Catholics and Protestants and given to the Church of Ireland clergyman. In the years leading to the Poor Enquiry, many people had refused to pay the cess and tithes and this explains the comment of Revd Edward Wilson, Church of Ireland vicar of Taghmon, who stated that deserted children had been supported by the church cess, 'but since that has ceased, we have no means of support'.[99] In the parish of Rathgarrue, Revd Chaworth Browne, the Protestant vicar, stated that one child was supported 'by application to the assizes'.[100] This suggests that the child's father was known and was being compelled by court order to support his child.

The largest number of children born to single mothers was in Mullingar, where Revd Gibson stated there were thirty but thought the Catholic clergy might have a more accurate estimate, 'as they christen them'.[101] J.P. Lyon, a magistrate in Mullingar, seems to have been offended to be asked about 'bastard' children, as he replied, 'Oh fie!' to the question.[102] The children of single mothers were reported to be supported by their mothers begging, though in a few cases it was stated that their 'reputed fathers' supported them. In the parish of Kilkenny West, Revd John Kearney, the parish priest, commented on single mothers that 'in many cases I have known the mothers to refuse parting with them though under the penalty of not being allowed a shilling for its nursing or maintenance'.[103] This suggests that single mothers would be offered some financial support if they gave up their child, but to whom the child would be given is not indicated.

In the witness sessions, there was some disagreement about the numbers of children born to single mothers. In Castletown Delvin, Laurence Henry JP and Michael Hope, a farmer, stated that the number was large, while Robert Morgan Tighe JP believed that the number was small. Revd Joseph Fitzgerald, the parish priest of Castletown Delvin, stated that there were 'not more than four' in the parish. In Killucan, Fr John Curran, the parish priest, stated that there were five single mothers with children in the parish.

The witnesses in most of the parishes agreed that single mothers never abandoned or 'destroyed' their children but that the children were neglected by their fathers. (This contrasts with the situation in Dublin at that time where infanticide and the abandonment of children were common.[104]) Witnesses in Killucan stated that marriage between the parents of a child conceived outside of marriage 'was frequently brought about by the interference of the clergymen'.

Witnesses stated that the children of single mothers were never supported by the parish. In some cases, the mothers 'applied for wages' – that is, sought financial support from the father of their child – through the courts. If the mother could prove a promise on the part of the father to support the child, she might get an order that the father pay part of his wages to support his child. But such orders were often ineffectual, as magistrates had no power to punish recalcitrant fathers who refused to pay. Lord Westmeath stated that 'punishment is never inflicted upon those who apply for wages, even though they may have had more than one illegitimate child'.[105] In some cases, the application for wages by the mother led the reputed father to marry the mother of the child. The witnesses in Castletown Delvin stated that, 'in a case of manifest seduction, the magistrates are glad to see it produce this result'.[106] In Multyfarnham, witnesses stated that 'a feeling of honour sometimes and, occasionally, the dread of the mother's friends induces subsequent marriages'.

Most single mothers supported themselves by begging and some by working. In Multyfarnham, the witnesses stated that some mothers worked to support the child, either by spinning or agricultural work during ten months of the year. In Castletown Delvin, a witness stated that the children generally begged until they were 14, at which age they became servants or labourers or entered the army. Witnesses in Benowen stated that in general the children did not grow up vagrants as they seldom remained with their mothers beyond the age of ten, when they were employed by farmers.

The single mothers reduced to begging mostly left their own parish to beg because, as a witness in Benowen stated, 'there is some objections to relieve them when they are known'.[107] In four of the five parishes, the witnesses believed that some mothers of illegitimate children were driven into prostitution. Witnesses in Benowen believed that some of the women became prostitutes, 'not from the difficulty of supporting themselves and their children, but because they are more open to temptation'.

The witnesses all agreed that whatever their means of survival, the single mothers mainly experienced extreme poverty. Dr Cotter in Ballynacargy stated that a woman who consulted him for 'general debility' had a 'well-grown child at her breast', which he described should be weaned at once; she answered it would be impossible, as she had no other food to give it. Cotter said that 'such instances are very frequent'.[108] In Castlepollard, the witnesses agreed that 'the scanty provision which the mother is able to obtain of course often injures the health of the child'. The witnesses in Castletown Delvin also agreed that the mother's poverty injured the health of both mother and child. In Killucan, the witnesses believed that when mothers were driven to vagrancy or prostitution 'the child suffers very much for want of proper care and nourishment'.

The treatment of single mothers by their community was commented on by witnesses in all parishes. Most witnesses agreed that single mothers were 'treated with contempt by women of her own class and a great portion of that feeling extends to the "bastard" who would not receive in marriage, unless much richer, the daughter of even a small farmer'. In Multyfarnham, the witnesses believed that a single mother would have 'the greatest difficulty in procuring a husband except in the few instances where the man has been paid to marry her'.[109] In Delvin, Mr Hope, a farmer, believed that prejudice against single mothers was diminishing 'as the fault became more common'.

The evidence given to the commission concerning the plight of the able-bodied out of work, those unable to work through sickness, single mothers with children and widows with children and those unable to work due to age, showed that many in those groups were driven to begging or vagrancy to survive. The prevalence of vagrancy was of particular concern to the commission, and the section of the report on vagrancy in Westmeath is the longest, as it is for most other counties. The questionnaires had two questions on the number of beggars in the respondents' parish and what alms they were given. A question was also asked whether labourers gave lodgings to beggars or other travellers and how much was charged for such lodgings.

In only three parishes did the respondents say there were no beggars and in most the answer was 'a few' or 'not many'.[110] Most beggars were not resident in the parishes examined. Revd James Murray, parish priest in Clonmellon, stated that there were very few beggars 'who are native to the parish. Such as subsist by begging are usually strangers'.[111] In Kilkenny West, the Protestant rector, Revd R.B. Bryan, stated that there were only twelve 'decided beggars' in his parish but that 'those who are beggars, except in name, are very numerous'.[112] By this he may have meant that some of the labourers were so poor that they frequently had to beg to survive. Revd John Kearney, parish priest of Kilkenny and Noughoval, stated that while there were only twenty resident beggars, their numbers swelled to one hundred during the summer when 'strolling beggars' arrived in the parish. In Drumcree, Revd Mr De Courcy, the Protestant vicar, reported 'a great many beggars rambling through the parish'.

Revd John Young, Protestant rector in Stone Hall, stated that 'strangers so frequently crowd the neighbourhood that I am quite unable to say the number who subsist by begging, who I am grieved to say are very numerous'.[113] Patrick Byrne Esq., in Castletown, stated that were thirty resident beggars 'who receive alms and provisions in the spring and summer season of scarcity' but that one hundred beggars visited the parish.

Most alms were given to beggars in the form of food, mainly potatoes and meal. Robert Dowdall JP reported from the parish of Newtown that 'alms are given in money by the rich and in provisions by the lower orders'.[114] Revd J. Dowling, parish priest of Multyfarnham, stated that 'alms are always given in food by the farmers and in food, clothing and money by the gentry'.

Respondents to the questionnaires stated that beggars were given lodgings by most labourers for no charge, but the beggars were expected to provide their own straw, which would have been begged from farmers, as bedding. The straw, when discarded, would be used as manure. Travellers, other than beggars, were accommodated by labourers at a charge of one or two pence per night. Revd William Peacocke, Protestant rector of Drumraney, explained that widows would take in 'strollers' and 'partake of what the stranger had that day got for charity'.[115] Peacocke stated that, in some cases, 'farmers gave meal or potatoes, which is eaten at the house where he lodges or sold for whiskey'.

In the oral hearings, witnesses were asked to estimate how many beggars there were in their parish and several distinguished between what might be called resident beggars and 'strolling tinkers' and those periodically reduced to begging because of circumstances. In Ballynacargy/Kilbixy, the witnesses thought that there were few resident beggars but many strolling vagrants. Witnesses thought that the reduction in vagrancy was due to emigration and the greater cheapness of food while Fr Mullen the parish priest thought that the 'habits of the people are also improved'.[116] Witnesses in Ballynacargy/Kilbixy, as in several other parishes, stated that during the summer months women from other places and their children came to beg as their husbands were absent in search of work. In Benowen, Fr Kearney, the parish priest, stated that 'bodies of tinkers go through the country often with two wives each, and a number of children, who beg in small parties'.

Labourers from the Ballynacargy area who went to England in search of work did not usually beg their way but 'brought their own provisions'.[117] This was also the case in the parish of Benowen. It was not the custom in the Ballynacargy area for the elderly to make over their little farms to their children and then go out begging. Those reduced to begging attributed 'their reduced condition to the loss of husbands and fathers and the general scarcity of employment'.[118] In Killucan, David Moore, a shopkeeper, stated that many beggars were reduced to mendicancy by 'the sub-division of land and the rack-rent system which renders the holder of land unable to give employment'.[119]

Hugh Morgan Tuite, a local landlord and recently elected O'Connellite MP, stated that many 40s. freeholders had, since the passing of an act depriving them of the franchise, been evicted from their holdings and become paupers. Tuite was referring to the act that, after Catholic Emancipation in 1829, had raised the property threshold

for voting to £10, thus depriving of the vote the 40s. freeholders who
had been the main supporters of Daniel O'Connell.[120]

In the parish of Benowen, witnesses stated that there were about
thirty resident beggars and three to four strangers for every local
beggar. The parish priest, Fr Kearney, believed that 'when potatoes
are from 1d. to 1½d. per stone, there is scarcely a stranger beggar to be
seen'.[121] Witnesses in Benowen stated that cottier tenants rarely resorted
to begging but when they were obliged to do so, they went outside
their own area. In Benowen, Peggy Kiernan, a beggar, stated that her
husband was in the next parish with four of their five children. Kiernan
explained that she and her husband had rented some land but were
dispossessed when the lease was up. She explained that her husband had
worked as a labourer 'but got sick through cold and hardship and want
of covering at night; he is now unable to work and if able, could not
support seven children on his earnings'.[122] In Moate, witnesses stated
that there were many beggars who had formerly earned their own
subsistence and whose destitution was due to 'bad seasons, failure of
crops, sickness etc. and consequent inability to pay rent'.

In Killucan, witnesses disagreed about the number of beggars,
with Revd Curran, the parish priest, claiming that there were 300 to
400 who begged sometimes, while a local landlord, Peter Purdon, said
there were only 70. The Killucan witnesses agreed that the problem
of vagrancy was most common from May to September because
potatoes were scarce in those months and that 'numbers of strange
beggars crowd in from Connaught'.[123] Those beggars were mainly the
wives and children of men who were employed in other parts of the
country or in England. The resident beggars 'live on the borders of
bogs where they can have fuel in plenty and can easily get ground on
which to build a cabin'.

The commission enquired how much assistance beggars were
likely to get by begging, and whether in food or money. Farmers gave
mainly potatoes while shopkeepers gave money. In Ballynacargy,
it was stated that an able-bodied beggar might get two stone of
potatoes per day and might on some days 'procure more food than
would be sufficient for his own consumption'.[124] Some families of
beggars divided into two groups and got more than if they presented
themselves as a single group. Infirm beggars would obtain more
than a 'stout-looking beggar'.[125] Peggy Kiernan stated that she got

plenty of potatoes to eat for herself and her children but often did not get enough milk to feed her infant. William Conlon, a farmer in Benowen, asserted that beggars who had slept in his house had collected during the day 'much more than each individual could consume'.[126] On the issue of what beggars did with the proceeds of begging surplus to their needs, Kiernan stated that she never had anything to spare, but Michael Feeney, 'a well-dressed beggar', stated that he bought tobacco and clothes. In Castletown Delvin, witnesses thought that some male beggars, having got enough potatoes to feed themselves, would accept only meal, which they sold. In Moate, witnesses agreed that farmers gave beggars between half and three-quarters of a stone of potatoes, while shopkeepers gave between 1s. and 1s. 6d. per week.

Revd Adolphus Drought, the Protestant curate in Castlepollard, stated that he had been told by the children of beggars that their mothers often collected six or seven stone of potatoes and sold their surplus to buy tea, tobacco and whiskey. Drought thought that the women spent their surplus income on 'dissipation' rather than clothes because if they were better dressed, they might get less by begging. This view was also held by Patrick Geraghty, a farmer in Benowen, who claimed to know a woman 'who begs in rags and has a good new cloak which she wears on Sundays'.[127] Patrick Geraghty stated that he would assist a well-dressed beggar before one in rags because he considered that the man in rags had sold his clothes to buy alcohol. Fr Kearney, parish priest of Benowen, shared Geraghty's view and opined that 'rags are no recommendation to beggars as people suspect either that the beggar is a drunkard or has money hoarded up'.[128] Kearney also claimed that he had seen a woman begging who appeared to have a disgusting sore on her face, but it was discovered that the appearance of a sore had been produced 'by squeezing a ribbon very tight across the face'.[129] In addition, Kearney asserted that he had known beggars to pinch their children to make them cry when begging, but that 'they are fond of their children in general'.[130] In Killucan, most witnesses stated that rags and sores were not 'fostered for the purpose of exciting pity', but David Moore, a shopkeeper, claimed that 'sometimes revolting exhibitions of maimed persons are to be seen at fairs, but these belong to a distinct and not numerous class'.

In Mullingar, where the beggars received mainly money, the witnesses claimed that some beggars were dissolute and were often seen drunk on the streets. Beggars in Mullingar, according to George Reeves, a shopkeeper, 'get a great deal from passengers on coaches, who give to get rid of their importunity'.[131] Reeves also thought that the town beggars 'drink as much whiskey as would support a family' and stated that town beggars did better than some 'decent housekeepers who are reduced by the fall of the times and who will rather starve than beg'.

Witnesses in most parishes agreed that the burden of supporting beggars fell mainly on farmers and shopkeepers and that 'the houses of the gentry are shut'.[132] The farmers gave mainly potatoes and meal while the shopkeepers gave money. Labourers, despite their own poverty, also gave beggars any potatoes they could spare. In Multyfarnham, witnesses stated that those farmers and labourers gave proportionately more than the wealthy, 'some witnesses say 100-fold more', and that 'very many stint themselves to supply others'.[133] In Benowen, Michael Feeney, a beggar, stated that 'the labourers give more than any, considering their means'.[134] The motivation for giving to beggars was stated by several witnesses to be religious. People gave charity 'for God's sake and expect to be rewarded to the extent of their charity'.[135] Some gave because of the fear of 'the beggar's curse', but in Multyfarnham the farmer witnesses stated that 'farmers are not such fools as to give from dread of a beggar's curse'.

Witnesses were asked whether beggars were involved in crime or 'outrages' (i.e., attacks on landlords). There was general agreement that few if any beggars were involved in outrages. George Drought, a police magistrate in Killucan, stated that 'men have been paid to commit murder, but such are never destitute persons'.[136] In Castletown Delvin, Mr Hope, a farmer, and Fr Fitzgerald, the parish priest, thought that outrages, when they occurred, were due to destitution resulting from dispossession, but Lord Westmeath thought they were due to 'political causes'.[137] Some witnesses stated that petty crime was common among beggars. In Benowen, Philip Lennon, a farmer, told of another farmer he knew who went upstairs to fetch potatoes for a beggar woman who in the meantime robbed him of some clothes, but beggars, Lennon believed, were 'for the most part incapable of any violence, as able-bodied men are seldom amongst them'.[138] Some witnesses claimed that diseases were spread by beggars through the custom of the poorer farmers and labourers giving them lodgings. Vagrants, according to a witness in Castletown Delvin, were 'constantly in the habit of circulating gossip, fabrications and superstitious absurdities'.

Most witnesses agreed that beggars had large families and while some stated that the rate of illegitimacy was no higher than among labourers, others disagreed. In Moate, witnesses stated that beggars were kind to their children and sometimes shared their collections with others more destitute than themselves. Many witnesses believed that, apart from 'strolling tinkers' and 'confirmed beggars', many people were driven to beg occasionally through lack of employment or other misfortunes.

In all parishes, witnesses agreed that the characters of beggars were rarely evaluated when giving them alms and that beggars were never punished for vagrancy. Most witnesses were opposed to 'rigorous measures' being taken against beggars and, in Benowen, some witnesses stated that, in addition to the expectation of Heavenly reward for giving to beggars, there was 'a kind of pleasure in relieving them'.

Witnesses stated that there were no 'houses of industry or mendicity institutions' nearer than Dublin. If such institution were available, witnesses in most parishes thought that no beggar would willingly take refuge in them, but Michael Feeney, a beggar in Benowen, when asked about a house of industry, said 'I would be very proud to have such a place to go to and to spend all my life in it; I am tired of wandering and am growing old and weak'.[139] In Moate, Patrick Mulvaney, a labourer, stated that he would rather starve than go into a house of industry.

On the question of whether beggars should be supported by a tax, some shopkeepers favoured the proposal, arguing that they would probably pay less in tax than they gave out in cash as alms. In Mullingar, witnesses stated that 'shopkeepers would give considerable sums to be rid of the annoyance of beggars; their trade is injured by it'.[140] In Ballynacargy/Kilbixy, witnesses, by contrast, thought that farmers and shopkeepers would not prefer to give a regular sum as by giving directly to beggars they 'can suit their charity to their convenience; besides, the giving away of some food every day seems of less consequence than a sum of money, though less in value'.

In addition to taking evidence directly, the assistant commissioners circulated questionnaires on economic and social conditions in the baronies examined. The questionnaires were sent to Catholic and Protestant ministers and to magistrates in the parishes studied. The questionnaires asked who were the landlords of cottages and cabins and what was the rent charged and the conditions under which the cottages were rented and whether 'duty labour' was required in addition to or in lieu of rent. A question was asked about the furnishing of cabins and whether two or more families lived in any cabins. Those questioned were also asked if the situation in their parish had improved or deteriorated since 1815 and whether the area was peaceable.[141] Questions were asked whether there were savings banks or pawnbrokers in their parish, and the number of public houses and the extent of illicit distillation in the area.

The answers to the question on who were the landlords of cabins reveal the complex system of sub-letting that prevailed in Ireland in 1833. In most cases the answer was 'farmers', 'the better class of farmers' or 'small farmers', though in some cases the landlords were described as 'the gentry of the country' or 'landed proprietors'.[142] Revd John Kenny, parish priest in the parish of Kilkenny West, gave a succinct description of the system of sub-letting when he stated that the landlords of cottages and cabins were 'middlemen of every grade, from the renter of 300 acres down to the man that rents but three, each has sub-let to others'.[143] Charles Arabin JP, a landlord in the parish of Ballymore, explained the legal framework of landholding in his reply: 'If by cottages or cabins is meant the cottier's cabin, it is plain the land occupier must [be] the landlord, and therefore in this case the landlord consists of the nobleman, gentleman and every gradation of farmer'.[144] In Mullingar town, J. Lyons JP stated of the landlords that 'some were very respectable; some the reverse'.[145] In Kilbeggan, Revd Edward Wilson, the Church of Ireland minister, described the landlords of the town as distillers and brewers, workmen and the low class of tradesmen.

The responses to the question on the rent of cabins indicated that the rent of a cabin without land varied between £1 and £1 10s. For a cabin with about half an acre of land, the rent varied from £2 to £4 depending on the quality of the land. In the parish of Ballyloughloe and Drumraney, the local Church of Ireland minister, William

Peacocke, stated that a labourer could pay £3 for 'a rood of ground with a straw hut upon it'.[146]

Revd Peacocke considered that rent of cabins was 'one of the great grievances' because in addition to paying rent the labourer 'works for this middleman at 6*d*. or 7*d*. per day and his children run all the messages and the wife spins so much flax gratis'.

In most parishes, the witnesses stated that labourers' cabins were mud-walled hovels with straw roofs, devoid of furniture except for a few stools and, in some cases, a table and dresser. The answer of Revd Michael Berry, parish priest of Clonard, was typical of most parishes: 'The walls are mud covered with straw, rushes or scraws; the furniture, a pot, some stools; seldom a chair. No bedsteads; some have bedclothes of the worst sort; many use the clothes they wear by day as covering by night'.[147] In the parish of Kilkenny West, Revd R. Bryan, the Church of Ireland minister, described the cabins in his parish as being 'of the worst description, scarcely any furniture. Seldom one bedstead, often useless; a straw mat and one blanket to each bed'.[148] In the parish of Rathconrath, the cabins were 'tolerable good, being built of lime and stone; the furniture but indifferent', while in the neighbouring parish of Piercetown, J.D. Meares, the local landlord, described labourers' houses as built of lime and stone but poorly furnished.[149] In the parish of Castletown, Patrick Byrne Esq. described the cabins as being 'of the worst description, with scarcely any furniture, except a couple of stools and a pot. The inmates generally lie altogether on straw on the ground, covered with only the clothes they wear by day, with only one bad blanket or quilt'.[150]

Most respondents answered that 'duty labour' was not imposed in addition to or instead of money rent. In Ballyloughloe and Drumraney, Peacocke stated that some widows were provided with 'hovels' free of rent by 'middle-men', but they labour as 'the poor woman's wheel is full of the flax of the farmer, she picks all his potatoes and generally wheels his turf'.[151] In Castlepollard, W.D. Pollard JP reported that some farmers let cabins to labourers and received the rent in labour, but that this was not common. In the parish of Kilkenny West and Noughoval, the parish priest, Revd John Kearney, stated that 'in very many instances I have known them (the labourers) to engage in work for the landlord at a lower rate on account of getting the cabin'.[152] In Ballymore, the parish priest, Revd

John Falloon, answered that 'there is no such thing as duty-labour, but the graziers etc. have a number of cottages on the skirts of their large farms who get their cabins at a lower rent and consequently have a lower rate of wages'.

There was a wide variety of answers to the question of how many cabins housed more than one family, ranging from 'none' or 'very few' in most parishes to 'instances too numerous to ascertain' according to Revd De Courcy, Protestant rector of Drumcree and Dysart. Overcrowding was mainly a problem in the towns and larger villages. Revd James Murray, parish priest of Killucan, reported that while he knew of no instance of two families sharing a cabin in the countryside, in Clonmellon, a village of 900 inhabitants, there were about 20 cases of two families sharing cabins. In Castlepollard, W.D. Pollard JP estimated that there were 35 houses 'having more than one family under the same roof' while in Killucan (population 8,746) the parish priest, Revd John Curran, stated that there were between 70 and 100 shared cabins. In the largely rural parishes of Clonard and Coralstown (population *c*.7,000) the parish priest, Revd Michael Berry, thought that there were about 150 shared cabins. In the parish of Castlelost, the Church of Ireland minister, Revd Samuel Lewis, reported that there was no instance of shared cabins in the parish, 'as the two families would never agree'.[153]

To the question of whether the condition of the poorer classes had improved or deteriorated since the end of the Napoleonic Wars in 1815 and whether the population of the parish had increased or decreased, most responses stated that the condition of the poor was either worse or unchanged and that the population had increased. Of 46 respondents to this question, 22 stated that conditions had deteriorated, 15 stated that conditions were unchanged and 9 stated that conditions had improved. Robert Dowdall JP, of Newtown, stated that conditions had 'improved beyond all calculation'.[154] Dowdall did not say why this was the case, and in neighbouring parishes respondents stated that conditions had either deteriorated or remained unchanged. More typical of the responses was that of Revd Michael Berry, parish priest of Clonard, who stated that 'nothing can be worse than the condition of the poorer classes at present'.

Several respondents who reported a deterioration in conditions gave as the cause the economic depression in Ireland after the ending of the Napoleonic Wars, which had led to a drop in demand for Irish food. The parish priest of Castletown Delvin, Revd J. FitzGerald, stated that conditions were 'decidedly worse since the peace of 1815, arising from small wages and want of employment'.[155] In a lengthy reply, Revd James Murray, parish priest of Clonmellon, stated that conditions had greatly deteriorated. He explained that he had not heard of 'superabundant population' during the war but that after the war agricultural prices had fallen, rents were not reduced, and some small farmers were evicted from their holdings and became labourers, increasing the supply of labour and therefore causing wages to drop. He stated that the towns and villages were 'much crowded by these unhappy beings who, for want of employment or having been ejected from their small farms, cannot procure cabins in the country parts'.[156] In the parish of Killucan, the parish priest, Revd John Curran, also reported that conditions were 'unquestionably worse since the peace of 1815, arising from small wages and want of employment'.[157] Curran also reported that the population was increasing.

In the parish of Kilkenny West, the Church of Ireland minister, Revd R. Bryan, stated that 'poverty and population have proceeded *pari passu* since 1815'.[158] Bryan reported an astonishing increase of 48 per cent in the population of his parish between 1821 and 1831, from 2,500 to 3,600.

The impact of the mechanization of the linen industry in Britain on Irish flax weavers was mentioned by several witnesses as causing poverty. Revd William Eames, Church of Ireland minister in Clonfad, stated that 'the failure of the linen trade has acted very injuriously to the poor'.[159] Owen Daly JP in Stone Hall/Multyfarnham stated that, before 1815, women were better off 'being employed in the manufacture of flax, which would not now pay the ground rent and labour'.

In answer to the question of whether their parish had been disturbed or peaceable since 1815, 26 of 48 witnesses stated that the parish had been peaceable. Of the 22 who reported disturbances, most stated that their parish was disturbed 'sometimes' or 'occasionally'.[160] Revd John Kearney, parish priest of Kilkenny West, stated that a decade earlier 'the Rockite system had prevailed, and mighty outrages were committed but for the past six years they have ceased'.[161] (The Rockites were a violent secret society named after a mythical Captain

Rock who engaged in 'outrages' or a campaign of beatings, arson and murders against landlords in the period 1820 to 1824, in response to near famine conditions due to poor harvests.[162])

Between 1830 to 1836 a mainly peaceful, but occasionally violent resistance to the payment of tithes to the Protestant clergy was waged in Ireland.[163] The Tithes War was most acute in the south-east and south-west of Ireland but it also occurred in Westmeath. The war was mentioned as a cause of disturbances by several witnesses. Revd Augustus Potter, Protestant rector of Rathconrath, stated that his parish had been 'very much disturbed since the year 1815; there is an apparent tranquillity at present, but not to be depended on; neither church cess nor tithes have been paid for at least two years; perhaps that may be the cause'.[164]

In the parish of Ballyloughloe and Drumraney, the Church of Ireland vicar, Revd William Peacocke, gave an account of the effect of the Tithe War on him when he stated that an anti-tithe protest at Moate had 'entered into resolutions threatening death to all who paid tithes'.[165] Peacocke stated that he was 'obliged to have two magistrates and 40 police to hold the vestry'.[166] (The vestry was a meeting of the Church of Ireland minister and lay churchwardens which would have been convened to levy tithes.) Peacocke noted that 'all my Catholic labourers were ordered to leave me, and they obeyed, and my flax cut at night and police in my house'.[167] He commented that 'half the labourers, if they worked honestly, would do the agricultural work' and said there was 'no manufactures, for what Englishman would be let live in the country'.[168] Peacocke remarked that 'you never will have Ireland tranquil while the British connexion exists'.[169] The only solution he could see to the increasing poverty was for the government to subsidise emigration.

The questionnaires elicited the information that there were public houses in all but one of the forty-eight parishes surveyed. John P. Haugh JP stated that in Killucan and Kinnegad there were 'so many I can't count. To a prodigious degree'.[170] The local Church of Ireland clergyman, Revd James Alexander, estimated that there were thirteen public houses in Killucan as well as numerous unlicensed premises, while the Catholic parish priest, Revd John Curran, thought there were ten. In the parish of Kilbixy, which included the village of Ballynacargy, James West JP reported that there were sixteen public houses for a population of 2,280. Seven witnesses reported illicit distillation in their parishes and five mentioned unlicensed premises or 'private houses' where alcohol was sold. In Mullingar, J. Lyons JP reported that he did not know how many public houses were in the town, but considered there were far too many and commented that 'the last act relating to publicans is, I think, very injudicious, as it prevents the magistrates from having any power to withhold a licence once granted'.[171]

The evidence given to the commissioners in Westmeath shows that a large proportion of the county's population, perhaps 25 per cent, were living in wretched conditions, often on the verge of famine. The commissioners identified the groups they considered likely to be poor, such as the able-bodied out of work, the old, the sick, widows and single mothers, all of whom suffered severe want for at least part of the year and most of whom had no support to rely on when in want, other than the charity of neighbours. While the plight of those groups was grim, the position of labourers who were able-bodied and employed was little better because they relied on producing potatoes on conacre land to pay their rent and feed themselves and their family. For several months of the year, when there was no paid work for them, and their stock of potatoes was exhausted, they had to seek work elsewhere, often leaving their wives and children to beg, until they returned.

In Ireland, as the commission wrote in its first report, 'the great proportion of the population about and amongst whom the inquiry was to be made are constantly fluctuating between mendicancy and independent labour'.[172] The enormity of the problem of poverty in Ireland was summarized by the commission's comment in its third report that

> to determine what measures might be requisite to ameliorate the condition of the poorer classes in Ireland required an investigation extending to almost the whole social and productive system; for the poorer classes in Ireland may be considered as comprehending nearly the whole population.[173]

# 6. The Poor Commission's reports[1]

The Poor Commission's enquiries were unique among such British government enquiries in the nineteenth century in taking evidence in public from all social classes and printing it verbatim. The commission published three reports on its work between 1835 and 1837. The first report, published in 1835, contained the huge amount of evidence collected in the parochial examinations held throughout the country and from answers to the questionnaires returned by local dignitaries on the nature and extent of poverty in Ireland. A shorter volume of extracts from the report was also published, and widely quoted in the press, but the absence of any recommendations for relieving the appalling level of poverty revealed by the report was criticized in the press.[2] The commission's second report on conditions in charitable institutions in Ireland was published in 1837 and contained no recommendations. Some critics saw in the second report hints that no public provision would be made for the destitute in Ireland and *The Times* demanded action to prevent the 'slow starvation' of the Irish poor as revealed in the evidence published in the second report.[3]

The commission's third report, which contained its recommendations, was finally delivered to the UK government in March 1836, after delays caused by disagreements between the commissioners and published in 1837. The most surprising aspect of the third report is that it makes very little reference to the huge collection of evidence published in the first report. As Niall Ó Ciosáin elucidates, the standard form of reports from commissions of enquiry instituted by the British government was to justify the commission's recommendations by reference to the facts collected.[4] The first eight pages of the third report contain an analysis of Irish poverty based largely on a comparison of the data in the 1831 censuses for Ireland and Britain, which could have been written without collecting the mass of evidence published in the first report. The only exception is the section recommending government-sponsored emigration, where nine pages are devoted to supporting the recommendation, by citing evidence collected in the oral hearings of many poor people's eagerness to emigrate.

The third report made recommendations on the categories of poor whose condition it had investigated as follows:

## A. THE ABLE-BODIED UNEMPLOYED

In making its recommendations, the commission was greatly influenced by the English Poor Law Amendment Act of 1834, which had reformed the poor laws that had operated from 1601. The principle underlying the reform was 'less eligibility', which required that assistance to able-bodied unemployed workers would be provided in workhouses where conditions would be worse than those experienced by the poorest labourers in the community. Entering a workhouse would thus be a last resort and unemployed workers would be driven to seek work elsewhere in England or to emigrate. The commission argued that implementing this principle in Ireland would be impossible because of the scale of unemployment. In its third report, the commission commented that 'the difficulty in Ireland is not to make the able-bodied look for work but to find profitable work for the many who seek it'.[5] Even if an Irish poor law, administered through workhouses, were possible, the commission rejected it on ideological grounds, pointing to the 'vicious tendency of any plan, however plausible, for securing to the whole of the able-bodied, a right to outdoor relief and support'.

The commission estimated that there were 585,000 people out of work for about thirty weeks of the year who, with their dependants, constituted 2,385,000 people in need of assistance. This calculation suggests that one third of the population of Ireland were destitute. To build workhouses to accommodate this number would have cost £4 million and to support them at the rate of 2½d. per day (the daily cost of supporting paupers in Dublin's Mendicity Institution) would cost £5 million per annum. The commissioners pointed out the enormity of this cost, relative to Ireland's resources, by noting that the total public revenue of Ireland was £4 million, while the net income of landlords was £6 million. The commissioners argued that the recently introduced workhouse system in England did not seek to put the able-bodied unemployed to work but to force them to migrate within England to seek employment. In Ireland, the commissioners argued, this policy would be futile given the mass unemployment of labourers throughout Ireland. The commission also rejected the suggestion that outdoor relief work be provided for the able-bodied unemployed, arguing that this too would be prohibitively expensive and that such systems had been tried in England and 'had not only failed but produced effects the very reverse of what were intended'.

### B. ASSISTED EMIGRATION AND AGRICULTURAL IMPROVEMENT

In view of the oversupply of labour, the commission's main recommendation for the relief of poverty in Ireland was government-assisted emigration. The commission noted that emigration was already occurring on a large scale and that most of those who left were eager to do so. The commission proposed that poor-law commissioners be empowered to borrow money to fund emigration. Emigrants assisted would have to repay the money given to them to fund their emigration to other parts of the British Empire under a scheme like the system of indentured labour introduced by the British in India in 1834, following the abolition of slavery. While the commission envisaged that most emigration would be voluntary, it proposed that vagrants and orphan children be compulsorily deported as indentured labourers. At the time the commission reported, vagrancy was a crime punishable by seven years transportation though this law was not widely enforced.

While the commission believed that the main solution to the problem of the oversupply of agricultural labour was emigration, it argued that emigration was to be 'auxiliary to commencing a course of amelioration' and therefore recommended various measures to achieve this amelioration. The commission considered that the agricultural labourers relying on conacre were 'so utterly unacquainted with any course of good cultivation that it is supposed they do not make the land they hold yield one third of the produce that it might under proper management'.[6] The commission proposed a system of agricultural training for these labourers and suggested the establishment of an agricultural model school in each parish. A board of improvement for agriculture would also fund land-drainage schemes and the cultivation of waste land, while a board of works would fund infrastructural projects, mainly roads and bridges.

### C. THE OLD, THE SICK AND THE DISABLED

The commission recommended that legal provision be made and a rate levied to support 'incurable as well as curable lunatics, idiots, epileptic persons, cripples, deaf-and-dumb and blind poor and all who labour under permanent bodily infirmities'.[7] This relief was to be provided 'within the walls of public institutions'.[8] The levying of rates to fund those institutions and their administration were to be carried out by poor-law commissioners. A board of guardians of the poor law would be elected by the ratepayers to direct the institutions for the relief of the poor.

The commission noted that 'mendicancy was the sole resource of the aged and impotent of the poorer classes' and that this led to the 'indiscriminate giving of alms, which encourages idleness, imposture and general crime'.[9] The commissioners disagreed on how to provide for 'aged and infirm, orphans, helpless widows with young children and destitute persons in general'.[10] Some commissioners thought that they should be supported fully by public funds, but a majority favoured a mix of private charity and public provision.

### D. IRISH LABOUR MIGRATION TO ENGLAND AND FOOD EXPORTS TO ENGLAND

The commission addressed two issues relating to poverty in Ireland that also affected England, namely agricultural exports and labour migration. English farmers at the time believed that the import of food into England from Ireland lowered the price they received and English workers complained that immigrant labour from Ireland lowered English wages. The commission was aware that a poor law had been proposed for Ireland in order that the 'Irish labourer stay at home and consume the corn he raises and that the English farmer have remunerating prices'.[11] The commission rejected this argument, pointing out that if food were not exported, Ireland could not import manufactured goods from the UK. The commission also argued that Irish labourers migrated to England to meet a shortage of labour and were well regarded by English employers as attested by some of those employers to the commission.

## E. INTEREST RATES, ALCOHOL AND THE TITHES

The commission had heard evidence of the extortionate interest rates that the poor paid to borrow money and proposed the establishment of a state loan fund to lend at low interest rates to the poor. The commission was also concerned at the problems caused by the consumption of 'ardent spirits' by the poor and recommended that access to alcohol be limited by prohibiting grocers from selling it.

At the time the commission was gathering evidence, the Tithes War was in progress and solutions to it were being discussed in parliament.[12] The tithes were a tax on agricultural output which, while mainly used to support the Anglican clergy, were also intended to be used to provide very minimal support for the destitute. The tithes fell most heavily on those least able to pay and, in the case of the poorest farmers and tenants, were collected in kind in the form of pigs and potatoes. Tithes were bitterly resented by Catholic farmers and some Protestant owners of small farms and in the period 1831–6 this resentment erupted into violence. The commission proposed that the British government buy the tithe composition (the capitalized value of future tithe income) and fund the purchase by the issue of government bonds. The fund purchased would be used to partly finance the institutions for the disabled and sick which were proposed. While this proposal was not enacted, a Tithe Commutation Act was introduced in 1838, which reduced tithes by a quarter with the remainder payable in rent to landlords.

When the huge amount of evidence collected by the commission showed that in Ireland the largest number of poor were labourers who were unemployed for several months of the year between sowing and harvesting, Whately and those who shared his ideology on the commission could only suggest emigration as the main solution to this problem. Whately's adviser and former student at Oxford, Nassau

Senior believed that only depopulation could solve Irish poverty and commented after the Famine that the million deaths from hunger and disease had 'scarcely been enough to do much good'.[13] During the Famine, Senior objected to the establishment of soup kitchens and the extension of the poor law to permit outdoor relief.

The most insightful analysis of the causes of Ireland's poverty is contained not in the commission's reports but in Appendix H Part II, written by commission member James Ebenezer Bicheno.[14] Bicheno saw that the subdivision of land and the conacre system, which had led to the creation of a vast number of impoverished agricultural labourers, was due to Ireland's form of land tenure with its absentee landlords and layers of middlemen engaged in sub-letting land. Sub-division of farms also led to early marriages and a high marriage rate among the poorest labourers. Bicheno argued, in relation to the early and improvident marriages, that 'their vices spring from their situation, not their situation from their vices'.[15] He observed that the Irish peasants were 'superior in intelligence, skill and enterprise' to the peasants of other European countries and 'their equals in industry, economy and virtue'.

Bicheno considered that a poor law, while it might mitigate the effects of poverty, would not address its causes. He argued that reform of land holding was vital for reducing poverty and pointed out that exhorting the peasants and the landlords to change their ways would have little effect unless reforms that changed the interests of both were introduced.

Had land-structure reform, as advocated by Bicheno, been implemented in the 1830s it is possible that the effects of the Famine would have been less severe. But the British government was unwilling to consider such reforms and only the disaster of the Famine would lead to an end to early marriages and subdivision of farms and to the bequeathing of farms to only one child, usually the oldest son, with other children having to leave the farm, the majority emigrating.

The plight of the large proportion of Ireland's population in the 1830s living on the verge of famine is an illustration of the entitlements theory of famine advanced by the Nobel-Prize-winning Indian economist, Amartya Sen.[16] Sen argued that many famines are caused not by a drastic reduction in the supply of food but by a

lack of entitlement to available food because of a fall in the output
of the subsistence food, a lack of income to buy available food or
the absence of food relief. In Ireland in the 1830s, most agricultural
labourers were entirely dependent for their food on the potatoes they
produced themselves. What little money they earned from working
for farmers for part of the year went to pay their rent. A failure of the
potato crop would therefore eliminate their sole entitlement to food
and plunge them into famine.

# 7. The implementation of the poor law in Westmeath

The reaction to the Poor Commission's recommendations was swift and largely negative. John Revans, who was secretary to the commission and had previously served as secretary to the English Poor Law Commission, which had recommended a workhouse-based poor law that was now in place, produced a lengthy pamphlet, *Evils of the state of Ireland*,[1] drawing extensively on the evidence collected by the commission, in which he called for an immediate introduction in Ireland of a modified version of the English poor law including some outdoor relief. Revans envisaged the establishment of five hundred 'houses of refuge' with the workhouse test only being applied to the able-bodied unemployed, while the old, the infirm and children would be given outdoor relief.

The home secretary, Lord John Russell, in 1836 asked George Nicholls, one of the architects of the new English poor law, and a permanent poor commissioner for England, to go to Ireland to investigate the feasibility of introducing an English-style poor law in Ireland.[2] Nicholls travelled to Ireland in 1837 and toured the country for six weeks to see for himself the extent of poverty and the feasibility of extending the English poor law to Ireland. In 1837 and 1838, Nicholls wrote three reports supportive of an Irish poor law. He argued that no lasting improvement was possible in Ireland until an end was put to the division of land into ever smaller holdings, which was forcing living standards down to subsistence level. Survival on such small patches of land was only possible because the holders could beg. A poor law would enforce a less attractive alternative to begging and therefore lead to consolidation of the smallest farms. Nicholls also argued that excluding the able-bodied poor from relief would not reduce agrarian violence, as the most likely perpetrators of such violence were able-bodied unemployed men.

In 1838 an Irish poor law was enacted, and Nicholls was appointed to oversee its implementation and the construction of a network of workhouses which were to be its core provision. Nicholls considered that workhouses to accommodate 80,000 people, or 1 per cent of the population, would be adequate. He used the figure of 1 per cent as this was the percentage of the people who were destitute in the most pauperized counties in England, namely Kent, Berkshire, Sussex and Oxfordshire. McCabe observes that in using the 'pauperized' English counties to estimate the numbers of destitute, Nicholls only counted those in workhouses and that if he had included people receiving outdoor relief in those counties, the percentage needing relief would have been 7.7 per cent.[3] Nicholls' estimate was only 3 per cent of the 2.3 million estimated to be living in poverty by the Whately Commission and, while the Whately figure may have been an overestimate, it was at least an attempt directly to estimate the numbers living in poverty.

The workhouse system introduced in England in 1836 was based on the principle of 'less eligibility', which required that the standard of living provided by the workhouse be less than that of the poorest labourer surviving outside the workhouse. On his tour of Ireland in 1837, Nicholls was taken aback at the abjectness of the poverty he saw, commenting that it would be impossible to make the lodging, clothing and diet of the inmates of an Irish workhouse worse than those of the majority of impoverished labourers. It would have been hard to devise a diet worse than that of the poorest Irish people in 1837. Yet on finding that the poor ate potatoes and milk for breakfast and dinner and had a supper only during occasional seasons of plenty, Nicholls decreed that the workhouse diet would consist of two meals, a breakfast of 8oz of stirabout (porridge) and half a pint of milk and a dinner of 3½lbs of potatoes and one pint of skim milk (fig. 5).

Nicholls oversaw the creation of 130 poor-law unions, which were groups of parishes centred on the major towns. The workhouses were situated in market towns, with most poor-law unions having a radius of about ten miles around the workhouse, though some in the west of Ireland were much larger. In response to the Famine, some of the larger unions were subdivided, with 163 being created eventually. The unions were governed by an elected board of guardians empowered to levy a poor-law rate based on property values.

5. Mullingar Workhouse (now St Mary's Hospital) opened in 1842

Two poor-law unions were established in Westmeath in 1839 centred on Mullingar and Athlone where workhouses were built.[4] A third, the union of Castletown Delvin (now Delvin), comprising parts of the Mullingar, Kells and Oldcastle unions, was added in 1850 and was the last union to be created in Ireland. A workhouse was built in Delvin. Mullingar poor-law union covered an area of 392 square miles and had a population of 68,102 according to the 1831 census, though by 1839 the population was significantly greater. Athlone poor-law union, which included a part of Roscommon, had an area of 382 square miles and served a population of 73,052 as recorded in the 1831 census. The workhouses in Athlone and Mullingar were both designed to house 900 inmates. Athlone's workhouse was completed and admitted its first inmates in 1841 while the workhouse in Mullingar was opened in 1842.

In setting up a workhouse-based poor law, Nicholls believed that the existence of the workhouse would put an end to begging and thereby end the conacre system of subdivision on which the poorest labourers could survive for several months only by begging. But the regime in the workhouses was so harsh that only the threat of immediate starvation would drive people into them. It was not until the potato crop failed in 1846, and the only food the landless labourers produced or could beg from people just a little better off than themselves was no longer available that they sought refuge in the workhouses. Though built to accommodate 900, in August 1843 there were only 369 inmates in Mullingar workhouse.[5] By May 1846, the number had risen to 440[6] but in November 1846 as the Famine began to take hold, the number had risen to 600 and by 1848 the workhouse would be overwhelmed with the number of inmates rising to 1,894,[7] necessitating the commissioning of two auxiliary workhouses in Mullingar.

The findings of the Poor Commission in Westmeath show that a large part of the county's population was living on the brink of famine. One of the most disturbing testimonies in Westmeath was that of Patrick Mulvaney, a labourer, who was described by an assistant commissioner as 'emaciated to a frightful degree and his face was greenish yellow', which the farmers said was invariably the consequence of living on 'prassagh' or wild mustard. Like many other labourers, Mulvaney was experiencing malnutrition. He explained that he faced starvation as he would not be permitted to dig his half-rood of potatoes because the owner of the land had distrained the crop to pay the rent. Like most of his fellow labourers, Mulvaney's only entitlement to food was what he could keep of the crop of potatoes he produced. If that crop failed, he and at least two million people in the same situation faced the inevitability of famine.

When the potato crop failed in 1846, the resulting famine led to a fall in the population of Westmeath of 21 per cent between 1841 and 1851, due to death and emigration, compared to a fall in the total population of Ireland of 13 per cent in the same period. O'Brien shows that the western fringe of Mullingar poor-law union was as badly affected by the Famine as the western seaboard of Ireland.[8] Byrne notes that the population of the western parish of Emper fell by 32 per cent between 1841 and 1851 and, together with three surrounding parishes, continued to fall up to 2016.[9] The poverty of pre-Famine Westmeath would cast its shadow into the twenty-first century.

# Notes

## ABBREVIATIONS

EPPI    Enhanced British Parliamentary Papers on Ireland
HC      House of Commons
HL      House of Lords
HMSO    His/Her Majesty's Stationery Office
MU      Maynooth University

INTRODUCTION

1   T.P. O'Neill, 'Poverty in Ireland, 1815–45', *Journal of Ethnological Studies*, 11 (1973), pp 22–33.
2   Wriothesley Noel, *Notes on a tour through the midland counties of Ireland, in the summer of 1836* (London, 1837), p. 127.
3   Gustave de Beaumont, *Ireland: social, political and religious* (Cambridge, MA, 2006), p. 462.

1. UNDERDEVELOPMENT AND POVERTY IN IRELAND, 1800–36

1   The commission's reports are most easily accessed in the EPPI at www.dippam. ac.uk by searching for Command Papers from 1835 to 1837 (accessed 23 Mar. 2023).
2   Joseph Lee, 'On the accuracy of the pre-Famine Irish censuses' in J.M. Goldstrom and L. Clarkson (eds), *Irish population, economy and society: essays in honour of the late K.H. Connell* (Oxford, 1981), pp 37–56.
3   Andy Bielenberg, 'The Irish economy, 1815–1880: agricultural transition, the communications revolution and the limits of industrialization' in James Kelly (ed.), *Cambridge history of Ireland*, 3, *1730–1880* (Cambridge, 2018), pp 179–203.
4   *Royal commission for enquiring into the condition of the poorer classes in Ireland, Third report, Appendix H, Part II*, HMSO 1836, available at www.dippam.ac.uk/eppi/documents/11048/page/252462.
5   Joel Mokyr, *Why Ireland starved: a quantitative and analytical history of the Irish economy, 1800–1850* (London, 1983).

6   P.M.A. Burke, 'The use of the potato crop in pre-Famine Ireland', *Journal of the Statistical and Social Enquiry Society of Ireland*, 21 (1959), pp 72–96.
7   Mokyr, *Why Ireland starved*.
8   Ibid.
9   Ibid.
10  Cormac Ó Gráda, *Ireland: a new economic history, 1780–1939* (Oxford, 1994).
11  Poor Commission, *First report* (1836).
12  Mokyr, *Why Ireland starved*.
13  Ó Gráda, *Ireland*.
14  Cormac Ó Gráda, 'Poverty, population and agriculture, 1801–1845' in W.E. Vaughan (ed.), *A new history of Ireland*, 5 (Oxford, 2010), pp 108–33.
15  Gustave de Beaumont, *Ireland: social, political and religious* (Cambridge, 2006).
16  Ibid., p. 462.
17  Henry Inglis, *A journey throughout Ireland during the spring, summer and autumn of 1834* (London, 1838).
18  Ibid., p. 153.
19  Ibid., p. 154.
20  Ibid., p. 193.
21  Ibid., p. 196.
22  Ibid.
23  Ibid., p. 195.
24  J.E. Bicheno, *Ireland and its economy: being the result of observations made in a tour through the country in the autumn of 1829* (London, 1830).
25  Ibid., p. 8.
26  Ibid., p. 123.
27  Ibid.
28  Ibid., p. 33.

29 Ciarán McCabe, *Begging, charity and religion in pre-Famine Ireland* (Liverpool, 2018).

2. POVERTY AND ITS RELIEF IN IRELAND, 1800–38
1 McCabe, *Begging, charity and religion*.
2 Ibid.
3 Ibid.
4 Ibid.
5 *First report from the select committee on the state of disease, and condition of the labouring poor in Ireland* (HC, 1823).
6 *Report of the select committee on the employment of the poor in Ireland* (HC, 1823).
7 *First report of the select committee on the state of Ireland* (HC, 1825).
8 Peter Gray, *The making of the Irish poor law, 1815–1843* (Manchester, 2009).
9 *Report of the select committee on the state of the poor in Ireland* (HC, 1830).
10 Gray, *The making of the Irish poor law*.
11 Ibid.

3. THE ESTABLISHMENT OF A ROYAL COMMISSION TO ENQUIRE INTO THE CONDITION OF THE POORER CLASSES IN IRELAND
1 Gray, *The making of the Irish poor law*.
2 Richard Whately, Sermon XIV: 'On Christ's example' in *Sermons on various subjects* (London, 1835).

4. SOCIAL UNREST AND POLITICS IN 1830S WESTMEATH
1 Seamus O'Brien, *Famine in Mullingar poor law union, 1845–9* (Maynooth, 1999).
2 Ibid.
3 Ibid.
4 G.E. Christianson, 'Secret societies and agrarian violence in Ireland, 1790–1840', *Agricultural History*, 46:3 (1972), pp 369–84.
5 Ibid.
6 Samuel Clarke, 'The importance of agrarian classes: agrarian class structure and collective action in nineteenth-century Ireland', *British Journal of Sociology*, 29:1 (Mar. 1978), pp 22–40.
7 John Kenny, 'Politics and society in Westmeath, 1815–1835' (MLitt., MU, 2015).
8 Ibid.

9 www.historyofparliamentonline.org/volume/1820–1832/member/tuite-hugh-1795–1868 (accessed 5 Apr. 2023).
10 *Westmeath Journal*, 8 June 1826.
11 www.historyofparliamentonline.org/volume/1820–1832/constituencies/co-westmeath (accessed 5 Apr. 2023).
12 Ibid.
13 www.historyofparliamentonline.org/volume/1820–1832/constituencies/co-westmeath (accessed 5 Apr. 2023).
14 *Westmeath Journal*, 29 June 1826.
15 www.historyofparliamentonline.org/volume/1820–1832/constituencies/co-westmeath (accessed 5 Apr. 2023).
16 O'Brien, *Famine in Mullingar*.
17 Ibid.
18 Patrick Casey, *The burning tower: the life and times of Sir Francis Hopkins, Bart (1813–1860), Westmeath landlord, socialite, traveller and romantic* (Dublin, 2020).
19 Ibid., p. 92.
20 Ibid., p. 94.
21 Niall Whelehan, 'Labour and agrarian violence in the Irish midlands, 1850–1870', *Saothar: Journal of the Irish Labour History Society*, 37 (2012), pp 7–18.
22 *Report of the select committee of the House of Lords on the state of Ireland* (HL, 1839).
23 O'Brien, *Famine in Mullingar*.
24 Casey, *The burning tower*.
25 *Westmeath Guardian*, 11 Apr. 1844.
26 www.duchas.ie/en/cbes/5009079/4984442/5119063.
27 Kenny, 'Politics and society in Westmeath'.
28 Ibid.
29 Ibid.
30 *Report of the select committee of the House of Lords on the state of Ireland* (HL, 1825).
31 Kenny, 'Politics and society in Westmeath'.
32 Ibid.

5. THE POOR COMMISSION'S INVESTIGATIONS IN WESTMEATH
1 *Royal commission for inquiring into the condition of the poorer classes in Ireland, First report, Appendix A* (HC, 1836), available at www.dippam.ac.uk/eppi/documents/10931 (accessed 27 Mar. 2023).
2 The modern spellings of place-names are used.
3 *Appendix A*, p. 407.

4 *Supplement to Appendix A,* p. 141, available at www.dippam.ac.uk/eppi/documents/10931/pages/246818 (accessed 5 Apr. 2023)
5 Ibid., p. 140.
6 Ibid.
7 Ibid., p. 141.
8 *Appendix A,* p. 409.
9 Ibid.
10 Ibid.
11 Ibid.
12 Ibid.
13 Ibid., p. 407.
14 Ibid., p. 409.
15 Ibid.
16 Ibid., p. 411.
17 Ibid., p. 408.
18 Ibid., p. 407.
19 Ibid.
20 Ibid., p. 410.
21 Ibid., p. 411.
22 Ibid., p. 408.
23 Ibid., p. 407.
24 Ibid., p. 408.
25 Ibid.
26 Ibid.
27 Ibid.
28 Ibid.
29 Ibid., p. 411.
30 Ibid., p. 409.
31 Ibid., p. 410.
32 Poor Commission, *Third report* (1836), p. 10, available at www.dippam.ac.uk/eppi/documents/11048 (accessed 31 Mar. 2023).
33 *Appendix A,* p. 411.
34 Ibid., p. 410.
35 Ibid.
36 Ibid.
37 Ibid.
38 Ibid., p. 220.
39 Patrick O'Donoghue, 'Opposition to tithe payment in Ireland', *Studia Hibernica,* 5 (1965), p. 80.
40 *Supplement to Appendix A,* p. 222.
41 Ibid., p. 223.
42 Ibid., p. 221.
43 Ibid., p. 223.
44 Ibid., p. 222.
45 Ibid., p. 580.
46 Ibid., p. 220.
47 Ibid.
48 Ibid.
49 Ibid.

50 Ibid., p. 221.
51 Ibid., p. 222.
52 Ibid., p. 223.
53 Ibid., p. 220.
54 Ibid., p. 222.
55 Ibid., p. 223.
56 Ibid.
57 Ibid., p. 221.
58 Ibid., p. 222.
59 Ibid., p. 223.
60 Ibid., p. 224.
61 Ibid.
62 Nigel Goose and Stuart Basten, 'Almshouse residency in nineteenth-century England: an interim report', *Family and Community History,* 12 (2009), pp 65–76.
63 *Appendix A,* p. 307.
64 Ibid., p. 308.
65 Ibid.
66 Ibid., p. 309.
67 Ibid.
68 Ibid., p. 310.
69 Ibid., p. 307.
70 Ibid., p. 309.
71 Ibid., p. 310.
72 Ibid.
73 Ibid., p. 308.
74 Ibid.
75 Ibid.
76 Ibid.
77 Ibid., p. 310.
78 *Supplement to Appendix A,* p. 141.
79 Ibid.
80 Ibid., p. 143.
81 Ibid., p. 144.
82 Ibid.
83 Ibid., p. 141.
84 Ibid.
85 Ibid.
86 Ibid., p. 142.
87 Ibid.
88 Ibid.
89 Ibid.
90 Ibid., p. 141.
91 Ibid., p. 142.
92 Ibid.
93 Ibid., p. 143.
94 Ibid., p. 134.
95 Ibid., p. 141.
96 Ibid., p. 135.
97 Ibid., p. 137.
98 Ibid., p. 134.
99 Ibid., p. 142.
100 Ibid.

101 Ibid., p. 141.
102 Ibid.
103 Ibid.
104 James Kelly, '"An unnatural crime": infanticide in early nineteenth-century Ireland', *Irish Economic and Social History*, 46:1 (2019), pp 66–110.
105 *Appendix A*, p. 69.
106 Ibid.
107 Ibid., p. 68.
108 Ibid.
109 Ibid., p. 70.
110 *Supplement to Appendix A*, pp 133, 132, 134.
111 Ibid., p. 136.
112 Ibid., p. 141.
113 Ibid., p. 134.
114 Ibid., p. 140.
115 Ibid., p. 134.
116 *Appendix A*, p. 577.
117 Ibid.
118 Ibid.
119 Ibid., p. 586.
120 P.M. Geoghegan, 'The impact of O'Connell' in *Cambridge history of Ireland*, 3, 1730–1880 (Cambridge, 2018), p. 112.
121 *Appendix A*, p. 579.
122 Ibid., p. 580.
123 Ibid., p. 586.
124 Ibid., p. 578.
125 Ibid., p. 580.
126 Ibid.
127 Ibid.
128 Ibid.
129 Ibid.
130 Ibid.
131 Ibid., p. 590.
132 Ibid.
133 Ibid., p. 592.
134 Ibid., p. 581.
135 Ibid., p. 579.
136 Ibid., p. 586.
137 Ibid., p. 584.
138 Ibid., p. 580.
139 Ibid., p. 582.
140 Ibid., p. 590.
141 *Supplement to Appendix A*, p. 1: www.dippam.ac.uk/eppi/documents/10931/pages/246818 (accessed 5 Apr. 2023).
142 Ibid., pp 126–35.
143 Ibid., p. 133.
144 Ibid., p. 135.
145 Ibid., p. 133.

146 Ibid., p. 126.
147 Ibid., p. 130.
148 Ibid., p. 133.
149 Ibid., p. 145.
150 Ibid., p. 142.
151 Ibid., p. 126.
152 Ibid., p. 133.
153 Ibid., p. 131.
154 Ibid., p. 132.
155 Ibid., p. 128.
156 Ibid.
157 Ibid., p. 130.
158 Ibid., p. 133.
159 Ibid., p. 131.
160 Ibid., pp 126–35.
161 Ibid., p. 133.
162 G.E. Christianson, 'Secret societies and agrarian violence in Ireland, 1790–1840', *Agricultural History* (1972), pp 369–84.
163 O'Donoghue, 'Opposition', p. 80.
164 *Supplement to Appendix A*, p. 145.
165 Ibid., p. 136.
166 Ibid.
167 Ibid.
168 Ibid.
169 Ibid.
170 Ibid., p. 130.
171 Ibid., p. 133.
172 *Royal commission for inquiring into the poorer classes in Ireland, First report*, HC (1836), p. 1: www.dippam.ac.uk/eppi/documents/10931/pages/246009 (accessed 5 Apr. 2023).
173 Ibid.

## 6. THE COMMISSION'S REPORTS

1 The commission's reports are most easily accessed at www.dippam.ac.uk/eppi by selecting Reports for the years 1835 to 1837.
2 Niall Ó Ciosáin, *Ireland in official print culture, 1800–1850: a new reading of the Poor Inquiry* (Oxford, 2014), pp 134–41.
3 Ibid.
4 Niall Ó Ciosáin, 'The Poor Enquiry and Irish society: a consensus theory of truth', *Transactions of the Royal Historical Society*, 9C (2010), pp 367–85.
5 *Third report*, p. 5, www.dippam.ac.uk/eppi/documents/11048/pages/252459 (accessed 5 Apr. 2023).
6 Ibid., p. 22.
7 Ibid., p. 25.

8  Ibid.
9  Ibid., p. 4.
10 Ibid., p. 25.
11 Ibid., p. 23.
12 Reid, 'The Tithe War in Ireland'.
13 Peter Gray, 'Nassau Senior, the *Edinburgh Review* and Ireland, 1843–49' in T.P. Foley and Seán Ryder (eds), *Ideology and Ireland in the nineteenth century* (Dublin, 1998), pp 130–43.
14 *Royal commission for inquiring into the condition of the poorer classes in Ireland, Third report*, Appendix H, Part II, HMSO 1836, available at www.dippam.ac.uk/eppi/documents/11048/page/252462 (accessed 5 Apr. 2023).
15 Ibid., p. 13.

16 A. Sen, *Poverty and famines: an essay on entitlement and deprivation* (London, 1981).

7.  THE IMPLEMENTATION OF THE POOR LAW IN WESTMEATH

1  Gray, *The making of the Irish poor law*.
2  John Revans, *Evils of the state of Ireland: their causes and remedy* (London, 1837).
3  McCabe, *Begging, charity and religion*.
4  workhouses.org.uk (accessed 5 Apr. 2023).
5  *Westmeath Guardian*, 24 Aug. 1843.
6  *Westmeath Guardian*, 20 May 1846.
7  *Westmeath Guardian*, 28 Dec. 1848.
8  O'Brien, *Famine in Mullingar*.
9  Seán Byrne, 'Emper: a Westmeath rural parish and its people in 1901', *Ríocht na Midhe*, 33 (2022), pp 163–95.